.0

Quick Start Guide

Get up to speed with the newly introduced features of
TensorFlow 2.0

Tony Holdroyd

BIRMINGHAM - MUMBAI

TensorFlow 2.0 Quick Start Guide

Commissioning Editor: Amey Varangoankar
Acquisition Editor: Shweta Pant
Content Development Editor: Kirk D'souza
Technical Editor: Sneha Hanchate
Copy Editor: Safis Editing
Project Coordinator: Namrata Swetta
Proofreader: Safis Editing
Indexer: Priyanka Dhadke
Graphics: Alishon Mendonsa
Production Coordinator: Aparna Bhagat

First published: March 2019

Production reference: 1280319

Published by Packt Publishing Ltd.
Livery Place
35 Livery Street
Birmingham
B3 2PB, UK.

ISBN 978-1-78953-075-9

www.packtpub.com

For my beautiful, talented wife, Sue McCreeth.

I absolutely love you.

Mapt

`mapt.io`

Mapt is an online digital library that gives you full access to over 5,000 books and videos, as well as industry leading tools to help you plan your personal development and advance your career. For more information, please visit our website.

Why subscribe?

- Spend less time learning and more time coding with practical eBooks and Videos from over 4,000 industry professionals
- Improve your learning with Skill Plans built especially for you
- Get a free eBook or video every month
- Mapt is fully searchable
- Copy and paste, print, and bookmark content

Packt.com

Did you know that Packt offers eBook versions of every book published, with PDF and ePub files available? You can upgrade to the eBook version at `www.packt.com` and as a print book customer, you are entitled to a discount on the eBook copy. Get in touch with us at `customercare@packtpub.com` for more details.

At `www.packt.com`, you can also read a collection of free technical articles, sign up for a range of free newsletters, and receive exclusive discounts and offers on Packt books and eBooks.

Contributors

About the author

Tony Holdroyd's first degree, from Durham University, was in maths and physics. He also has technical qualifications, including MCSD, MCSD.net, and SCJP. He holds an MSc in computer science from London University. He was a senior lecturer in computer science and maths in further education, designing and delivering programming courses in many languages, including C, C+, Java, C#, and SQL. His passion for neural networks stems from research he did for his MSc thesis. He has developed numerous machine learning, neural network, and deep learning applications, and has advised in the media industry on deep learning as applied to image and music processing. Tony lives in Gravesend, Kent, UK, with his wife, Sue McCreeth, who is a renowned musician.

I would like to thank the entire team behind this book at Packt, especially editors Kirk D'Souza, Sneha Hanchate, and Ayaan Hoda, as well as the graphics coordinator, Alishon Mendonsa.

I would also like to thank Peter Osborne, who gave me my first introduction and break into the wonderful world of computing.

About the reviewers

Sujit Pal is a technology research director at Elsevier Labs, an advanced technology group within the Reed-Elsevier Group of companies. His areas of interests include semantic research, **Natural Language Processing** (**NLP**), machine learning, and deep learning. At Elsevier, he has worked on several machine learning initiatives involving large image and text corpora, and other initiatives concerning recommendation systems and knowledge graph development. He has co-authored a book called *Deep Learning with Keras* with Antonio Gulli, and writes about technology on his blog, *Salmon Run*.

Narotam Singh recently took voluntary retirement from his post of meteorologist with the Indian Meteorological Department, Ministry of Earth Sciences, to pursue his dream of learning and helping society. He has been actively involved with various technical programs and the training of GOI officers in the field of IT and communication. He did his master's in the field of electronics, having graduated with a degree in physics. He also holds a diploma and a postgraduate diploma in the field of computer engineering. Presently, he works as a freelancer. He has many research publications to his name and has also served as a technical reviewer for numerous books. His present research interests involve AI, ML, DL, robotics, and spirituality.

Packt is searching for authors like you

If you're interested in becoming an author for Packt, please visit authors.packtpub.com and apply today. We have worked with thousands of developers and tech professionals, just like you, to help them share their insight with the global tech community. You can make a general application, apply for a specific hot topic that we are recruiting an author for, or submit your own idea.

Table of Contents

Preface

TensorFlow is one of the most popular machine learning frameworks in Python. With this book, you will improve your knowledge of the latest features of TensorFlow, and will be able to perform supervised and unsupervised machine learning using Python.

Who this book is for

As its title suggests, this book has been written to introduce readers to TensorFlow and many of its latest features, up to and including version 2.0.0 alpha, including eager execution, `tf.data`, `tf.keras`, TensorFlow Hub, machine learning, and neural network applications.

This book is intended to be useful for anyone with some exposure to machine learning and its applications: data scientists, machine learning engineers, computer scientists, computer science students, and hobbyists.

What this book covers

Chapter 1, *Introducing TensorFlow 2*, introduces TensorFlow by looking at a number of snippets of code, illustrating some basic operations. We will have an overview of the modern TensorFlow ecosystem and will see how to install TensorFlow.

Chapter 2, *Keras, a High-Level API for TensorFlow 2*, takes a look at the Keras API, including some general comments and insights, followed by a basic architecture expressed in four different ways, for training with the MNIST dataset.

Chapter 3, *ANN Technologies Using TensorFlow 2*, examines a number of technologies that support the creation and use of neural networks. This chapter will cover data presentation to an ANN, layers of an ANN, creating the model, gradient calculations for gradient descent algorithms, loss functions, and saving and restoring models.

Chapter 4, *Supervised Machine Learning Using TensorFlow 2*, describes examples of the use of TensorFlow for two situations involving linear regression where features are mapped to known labels that have continuous values, allowing predictions on unseen features to be made.

Chapter 5, *Unsupervised Learning Using TensorFlow 2*, looks at two applications of autoencoders in unsupervised learning: firstly for compressing data; and secondly, for denoising, in other words, removing noise from images.

Chapter 6, *Recognizing Images with TensorFlow 2*, firstly looks at the Google Quick Draw 1 image dataset, and secondly, at the CIFAR 10 image dataset.

Chapter 7, *Neural Style Transfer Using TensorFlow 2*, explains how to take a content image and a style image and then produce a hybrid image. We will use layers from the trained VGG19 model to accomplish this.

Chapter 8, *Recurrent Neural Networks Using TensorFlow 2*, initially discusses the general principles of RNNs and then looks at how to acquire and prepare some text for use by a model.

Chapter 9, *TensorFlow Estimators and TensorFlow Hub*, firstly looks at an estimator for training the fashion dataset. We will see how estimators provide a simple, intuitive API for TensorFlow. We will also look at a neural network for analyzing the film feedback database, IMDb.

Appendix, *Converting from tf1.12 to tf2*, contains some tips for converting your tf1.12 files to tf2.

To get the most out of this book

Working knowledge of Python 3.6 is assumed, as is familiarity with the use of Jupyter Notebooks.

The book is written assuming that readers are happier with explanations given in the form of code snippets and complete programs than long textual explanations, which, of course, have their place in different styles of book.

Some familiarity with machine learning concepts and techniques is highly recommended, although not absolutely essential if the reader is willing to do a little reading around on the subjects.

Download the example code files

You can download the example code files for this book from your account at www.packt.com. If you purchased this book elsewhere, you can visit www.packt.com/support and register to have the files emailed directly to you.

You can download the code files by following these steps:

1. Log in or register at `www.packt.com`.
2. Select the **SUPPORT** tab.
3. Click on **Code Downloads & Errata**.
4. Enter the name of the book in the **Search** box and follow the onscreen instructions.

Once the file is downloaded, please make sure that you unzip or extract the folder using the latest version of:

- WinRAR/7-Zip for Windows
- Zipeg/iZip/UnRarX for Mac
- 7-Zip/PeaZip for Linux

The code bundle for the book is also hosted on GitHub at `https://github.com/PacktPublishing/Tensorflow-2.0-Quick-Start-Guide`. In case there's an update to the code, it will be updated on the existing GitHub repository.

We also have other code bundles from our rich catalogue of books and videos available at `https://github.com/PacktPublishing/`. Check them out!

Download the color images

We also provide a PDF file that has color images of the screenshots/diagrams used in this book. You can download it here: `http://www.packtpub.com/sites/default/files/downloads/9781789530759_ColorImages.pdf`.

Conventions used

There are a number of text conventions used throughout this book.

`CodeInText`: Indicates code words in text, database table names, folder names, filenames, file extensions, pathnames, dummy URLs, user input, and Twitter handles. Here is an example: "Mount the downloaded `WebStorm-10*.dmg` disk image file as another disk in your system."

A block of code is set as follows:

```
image1 = tf.zeros([7, 28, 28, 3]) #  example-within-batch by height by
width by color
```

When we wish to draw your attention to a particular part of a code block, the relevant lines or items are set in bold:

```
r1 = tf.reshape(t2,[2,6]) # 2 rows 6 cols
r2 = tf.reshape(t2,[1,12]) # 1 rows 12 cols
r1
# <tf.Tensor: id=33, shape=(2, 6), dtype=float32,
numpy= array([[ 0., 1., 2., 3., 4., 5.], [ 6., 7., 8., 9., 10., 11.]],
dtype=float32)>
```

Any command-line input or output is written as follows:

```
var = tf.Variable([3, 3])
```

Bold: Indicates a new term, an important word, or words that you see on screen. For example, words in menus or dialog boxes appear in the text like this. Here is an example: "Select **System info** from the **Administration** panel."

Warnings or important notes appear like this.

Tips and tricks appear like this.

Get in touch

Feedback from our readers is always welcome.

General feedback: If you have questions about any aspect of this book, mention the book title in the subject of your message and email us at customercare@packtpub.com.

Errata: Although we have taken every care to ensure the accuracy of our content, mistakes do happen. If you have found a mistake in this book, we would be grateful if you would report this to us. Please visit www.packt.com/submit-errata, selecting your book, clicking on the Errata Submission Form link, and entering the details.

Piracy: If you come across any illegal copies of our works in any form on the internet, we would be grateful if you would provide us with the location address or website name. Please contact us at copyright@packt.com with a link to the material.

If you are interested in becoming an author: If there is a topic that you have expertise in, and you are interested in either writing or contributing to a book, please visit authors.packtpub.com.

Reviews

Please leave a review. Once you have read and used this book, why not leave a review on the site that you purchased it from? Potential readers can then see and use your unbiased opinion to make purchase decisions, we at Packt can understand what you think about our products, and our authors can see your feedback on their book. Thank you!

For more information about Packt, please visit packt.com.

Section 1: Introduction to TensorFlow 2.00 Alpha

In this section, we will introduce TensorFlow 2.00 alpha. We will begin with an overview of the major features of this machine learning ecosystem and see some examples of its use. We will then introduce TensorFlow's high-level Keras API. We will end the section with an investigation of artificial neural network technologies and techniques.

This section contains the following chapters:

- Chapter 1, *Introducing TensorFlow 2*
- Chapter 2, *Keras, a High-Level API for TensorFlow 2*
- Chapter 3, *ANN Technologies Using TensorFlow 2*

Introducing TensorFlow 2

TensorFlow began its life in 2011 as DisBelief, an internal, closed source project at Google. DisBelief was a machine learning system that employed deep learning neural networks. This system morphed into TensorFlow, which was released to the developer community under an Apache 2.0 open source license, on November 9, 2015. Version 1.0.0 made its appearance on February 11, 2017. There have been a number of point releases since then that have incorporated a wealth of new features.

At the time of writing this book, the most recent version is TensorFlow 2.0.0 alpha release, which was announced at the TensorFlow Dev Summit on March 6, 2019.

TensorFlow takes its name from, well, tensors. A tensor is a generalization of vectors and matrices to possibly higher dimensions. The rank of a tensor is the number of indices it takes to uniquely specify each element of that tensor. A scalar (a simple number) is a tensor of rank 0, a vector is a tensor of rank 1, a matrix is a tensor of rank 2, and a 3-dimensional array is a tensor of rank 3. A tensor has a datatype and a shape (all of the data items in a tensor must have the same type). An example of a 4-dimensional tensor (that is, rank 4) is an image where the dimensions are an example within—`batch`, `height`, `width`, and `color` channel (for example):

```
image1 = tf.zeros([7, 28, 28, 3]) # example-within-batch by height by
width by color
```

Although TensorFlow can be leveraged for many areas of numerical computing in general, and machine learning in particular, its main area of research and development has been in the applications of **Deep Neural Networks (DNN)**, where it has been used in diverse areas such as voice and sound recognition, for example, in the now widespread voice-activated assistants; text-based applications such as language translators; image recognition such as exo-planet hunting, cancer detection, and diagnosis; and time series applications such as recommendation systems.

In this chapter, we will discuss the following:

- Looking at the modern TensorFlow ecosystem
- Installing TensorFlow
- Housekeeping and eager operations
- Providing useful TensorFlow operations

Looking at the modern TensorFlow ecosystem

Let's discuss **eager execution**. The first incarnation of TensorFlow involved constructing a computational graph made up of operations and tensors, which had to be subsequently evaluated in what Google termed as session (this is known as declarative programming). This is still a common way to write TensorFlow programs. However, eager execution, available from release 1.5 onward in research form and baked into TensorFlow proper from release 1.7, involves the immediate evaluation of operations, with the consequence that tensors can be treated like NumPy arrays (this is known as imperative programming).

Google says that eager execution is the preferred method for research and development but that computational graphs are to be preferred for serving TensorFlow production applications.

`tf.data` is an API that allows you to build complicated data input pipelines from simpler, reusable parts. The highest level abstraction is `Dataset`, which comprises both elements of nested structures of tensors and a plan of transformations that are to act on those elements. There are classes for the following:

- There's `Dataset` consisting of fixed length record sets from at least one binary file (`FixedLengthRecordDataset`)
- There's `Dataset` consisting of records from at least one TFRecord file (`TFRecordDataset`)
- There's `Dataset` consisting of records that are lines from at least one text file (`TFRecordDataset`)
- There is also a class that represents the state of iterating through `Dataset` (`tf.data.Iterator`)

Let's move on to the **estimator**, which is a high-level API that allows you to build greatly simplified machine learning programs. Estimators take care of training, evaluation, prediction, and exports for serving.

TensorFlow.js is a collection of APIs that allow you to build and train models using either the low-level JavaScript linear algebra library or the high-level layers API. Hence, models can be trained and run in a browser.

TensorFlow Lite is a lightweight version of TensorFlow for mobile and embedded devices. It consists of a runtime interpreter and a set of utilities. The idea is that you train a model on a higher-powered machine and then convert your model into the .tflite format using the utilities. You then load the model into your device of choice. At the time of writing, TensorFlow Lite is supported on Android and iOS with a C++ API and has a Java wrapper for Android. If an Android device supports the **Android Neural Networks** (**ANN**) API for hardware acceleration, then the interpreter will use this, or else it will default to the CPU for execution.

TensorFlow Hub is a library designed to foster the publication, discovery, and use of reusable modules of machine learning models. In this context, a module is a self-contained piece of a TensorFlow graph together with its weights and other assets. The module can be reused in different tasks in a method known as transfer learning. The idea is that you train a model on a large dataset and then re-purpose the appropriate module for your different but related task. This approach brings a number of advantages—you can train a model with a smaller dataset, you can improve generalization, and you can significantly speed up training.

For example, the ImageNet dataset, together with a number of different neural network architectures such as inception_v3, has been very successfully used to jump-start many other image processing training problems.

TensorFlow Extended (**TFX**) is a TensorFlow-based general-purpose machine learning platform. Libraries released to open source to date include TensorFlow Transform, TensorFlow Model Analysis, and TensorFlow Serving.

tf.keras is a high-level neural networks API, written in Python, that interfaces to TensorFlow (and various other tensor tools). tf.keras supports fast prototyping and is user friendly, modular, and extensible. It supports both convolutional and recurrent networks and will run on CPUs and GPUs. Keras is the API of choice for developing in TensorFlow 2.

TensorBoard is a suite of visualization tools supporting the understanding, debugging, and optimizing of TensorFlow programs. It is compatible with both eager and graph execution environments. You can use TensorBoard to visualize various metrics of your model during training.

One recent development, and at the time of writing still very much in experimental form, integrates TensorFlow directly into the Swift programming language. TensorFlow applications in Swift are written using imperative code, that is, code that executes eagerly (at runtime). The Swift compiler automatically turns this source code into one TensorFlow Graph and this compiled code then executes with the full performance of TensorFlow Sessions on CPU, GPU, and TPU.

In this book, we will focus on those TensorFlow tools that allow us to get up and running with TensorFlow, using Python 3.6 and TensorFlow 2.0.0 alpha release. In particular, we will use eager execution as opposed to computational graphs and we will leverage the power of `tf.keras` for building networks wherever possible, as it is the modern way for research and experiment.

Installing TensorFlow

The best programming support for TensorFlow is provided for Python (although libraries do exist for Java, C, and Go, while those for other languages are under active development).

There is a wealth of information on the web for installing TensorFlow for Python.

It is standard practice, also recommended by Google, to install TensorFlow in a virtual environment, that is, an environment that isolates a set of APIs and code from other APIs and code and from the system-wide environment.

There are two distinct versions of TensorFlow—one for execution on a CPU and another for execution on a GPU. This last requires that the numerical libraries CUDA and CuDNN are installed. Tensorflow will default to GPU execution where possible. See `https://www.tensorflow.org/alpha/guide/using_gpu`.

Rather than attempt to reinvent the wheel here, there follow resources for creating virtual environments and installing TensorFlow.

In summary, TensorFlow may be installed for Windows 7 or later, Ubuntu Linux 16.04 or later, and macOS 10.12.6 or later.

There is a thorough introduction to virtual environments at
`http://docs.python-guide.org/`.

There is a very detailed set of information on all aspects of what is required to install TensorFlow in the official Google documentation at
`https://www.tensorflow.org/install/`.

Once installed, you can check your TensorFlow installation from a command terminal. There are instructions for doing this at `http://www.laurencemoroney.com/tensorflow-to-gpu-or-not-to-gpu/` and for installing the nightly build of TensorFlow, which contains all of the latest updates.

Housekeeping and eager operations

We will first look at how to import TensorFlow, then TensorFlow coding style, and how to do some basic housekeeping. After this, we will look at some basic TensorFlow operations. You can either create a Jupyter Notebook for these snippets or use your favorite IDE to create your source code. The code is all available in the GitHub repository.

Importing TensorFlow

Importing TensorFlow is straightforward. Note a couple of system checks:

```
import tensorflow as tf
print("TensorFlow version: {}".format(tf.__version__))
print("Eager execution is: {}".format(tf.executing_eagerly()))
print("Keras version: {}".format(tf.keras.__version__))
```

Coding style convention for TensorFlow

For Python applications, Google adheres to the PEP8 standard conventions. In particular, they use CamelCase for classes (for example, `hub.LatestModuleExporter`) and `snake_case` for functions, methods, and properties (for example, `tf.math.squared_difference`). Google also adheres to the Google Python Style Guide, which can be found at `https://github.com/google/styleguide/blob/gh-pages/pyguide.md`.

Using eager execution

Eager execution is the default in TensorFlow 2 and, as such, needs no special setup.

The following code can be used to find out whether a CPU or GPU is in use and if it's a GPU, whether that GPU is #0.

We suggest typing the code in rather than using copy and paste; this way you will get a feel for the commands:

```
var = tf.Variable([3, 3])

if tf.test.is_gpu_available():
    print('Running on GPU')
    print('GPU #0?')
    print(var.device.endswith('GPU:0'))
else:
    print('Running on CPU')
```

Declaring eager variables

The way to declare a TensorFlow eager variable is as follows:

```
t0 = 24 # python variable
t1 = tf.Variable(42) # rank 0 tensor
t2 = tf.Variable([ [ [0., 1., 2.], [3., 4., 5.] ], [ [6., 7., 8.], [9.,
10., 11.] ] ]) #rank 3 tensor
t0, t1, t2
```

The output will be as follows:

```
(24,
 <tf.Variable 'Variable:0' shape=() dtype=int32, numpy=42>,
 <tf.Variable 'Variable:0' shape=(2, 2, 3) dtype=float32, numpy=
 array([[[ 0.,   1.,   2.],
         [ 3.,   4.,   5.]],
        [[ 6.,   7.,   8.],
         [ 9., 10.,  11.]]], dtype=float32)>)
```

TensorFlow will infer the datatype, defaulting to `tf.float32` for floats and `tf.int32` for integers (see the preceding examples).

Alternatively, the datatype can be explicitly specified, as here:

```
f64 = tf.Variable(89, dtype = tf.float64)
f64.dtype
```

TensorFlow has a large number of built-in datatypes.

Examples include those seen previously, tf.int16, tf.complex64, and tf.string. See https://www.tensorflow.org/api_docs/python/tf/dtypes/DType. To reassign a variable, use var.assign(), as here:

```
f1 = tf.Variable(89.)
f1

# <tf.Variable 'Variable:0' shape=() dtype=float32, numpy=89.0>

f1.assign(98.)
f1

# <tf.Variable 'Variable:0' shape=() dtype=float32, numpy=98.0>
```

Declaring TensorFlow constants

TensorFlow constants may be declared as in the following example:

```
m_o_l = tf.constant(42)

m_o_l

# <tf.Tensor: id=45, shape=(), dtype=int32, numpy=42>

m_o_l.numpy()

# 42
```

Again, TensorFlow will infer the datatype, or it can be explicitly specified, as is the case with variables:

```
unit = tf.constant(1, dtype = tf.int64)

unit

# <tf.Tensor: id=48, shape=(), dtype=int64, numpy=1>
```

Shaping a tensor

The shape of a tensor is accessed via a property (rather than a function):

```
t2 = tf.Variable([ [ [0., 1., 2.], [3., 4., 5.] ], [ [6., 7., 8.], [9.,
10., 11.] ] ]) # tensor variable
print(t2.shape)
```

The output will be as follows:

```
(2, 2, 3)
```

Tensors may be reshaped and retain the same values, as is often required for constructing neural networks.

Here is an example:

```
r1 = tf.reshape(t2,[2,6]) # 2 rows 6 cols
r2 = tf.reshape(t2,[1,12]) # 1 rows 12 cols
r1
# <tf.Tensor: id=33, shape=(2, 6), dtype=float32,
numpy= array([[ 0., 1., 2., 3., 4., 5.], [ 6., 7., 8., 9., 10., 11.]],
dtype=float32)>
```

Here is another example:

```
r2 = tf.reshape(t2,[1,12]) # 1 row 12 columns
r2
# <tf.Tensor: id=36, shape=(1, 12), dtype=float32,
numpy= array([[ 0., 1., 2., 3., 4., 5., 6., 7., 8., 9., 10., 11.]],
dtype=float32)>
```

Ranking (dimensions) of a tensor

The rank of a tensor is the number of dimensions it has, that is, the number of indices that are required to specify any particular element of that tensor.

The rank of a tensor can be ascertained with this, for example:

```
tf.rank(t2)
```

The output will be as follows:

```
<tf.Tensor: id=53, shape=(), dtype=int32, numpy=3>
(the shape is () because the output here is a scalar value)
```

Specifying an element of a tensor

Specifying an element of a tensor is performed, as you would expect, by specifying the required indices.

Take this, for example:

```
t3 = t2[1, 0, 2] # slice 1, row 0, column 2
t3
```

The output will be as follows:

```
<tf.Tensor: id=75, shape=(), dtype=float32, numpy=8.0>
```

Casting a tensor to a NumPy/Python variable

Should you need to, you can cast a tensor to a numpy variable as follows:

```
print(t2.numpy())
```

The output will be as follows:

```
[[[ 0. 1. 2.] [ 3. 4. 5.]] [[ 6. 7. 8.] [ 9. 10. 11.]]]
```

Take this, also:

```
print(t2[1, 0, 2].numpy())
```

The output will be as follows:

```
8.0
```

Finding the size (number of elements) of a tensor

The number of elements in a tensor is easily obtained. Notice also, again, the use of the `.numpy()` function to extract the Python value from the tensor:

```
s =  tf.size(input=t2).numpy()
s
```

The output will be as follows:

```
12
```

Finding the datatype of a tensor

TensorFlow supports all of the datatypes you would expect. A full list is available at `https://www.tensorflow.org/versions/r1.1/programmers_guide/dims_types` and includes `tf.int32` (the default integer type), `tf.float32` (the default floating point type), and `tf.complex64` (the complex type).

To find the datatype of a tensor, use the following `dtype` property:

```
t3.dtype
```

The output will be as follows:

```
tf.float32
```

Specifying element-wise primitive tensor operations

Element-wise primitive tensor operations are specified using, as you would expect, the overloaded operators +, −, *, and /, as here:

```
t2*t2
```

The output will be as follows:

```
<tf.Tensor: id=555332, shape=(2, 2, 3), dtype=float32, numpy= array([[[ 0.,
1., 4.], [ 9., 16., 25.]], [[ 36., 49., 64.], [ 81., 100., 121.]]],
dtype=float32)>
```

Broadcasting

Element-wise tensor operations support broadcasting in the same way that NumPy arrays do. The simplest example is that of multiplying a tensor by a scalar:

```
t4 = t2*4
print(t4)
```

The output will be as follows:

```
tf.Tensor( [[[ 0. 4. 8.] [12. 16. 20.]] [[24. 28. 32.] [36. 40. 44.]]],
shape=(2, 2, 3), dtype=float32)
```

In this example, the scalar multiplier 4 is—conceptually, at least—expanded into an array that can be multiplied element-wise with t2. There is a very detailed discussion of broadcasting at `https://docs.scipy.org/doc/numpy/user/basics.broadcasting.html`.

Transposing TensorFlow and matrix multiplication

To transpose a matrix and matrix multiplication eagerly, use the following:

```
u = tf.constant([[3,4,3]])
v = tf.constant([[1,2,1]])
tf.matmul(u, tf.transpose(a=v))
```

The output will be as follows:

```
<tf.Tensor: id=555345, shape=(1, 1), dtype=int32, numpy=array([[14]],
dtype=int32)>
```

Note, again, that the default integer type is tf.int32 and the default float type is tf.float32.

All of the operations that are available for tensors that form part of a computational graph are also available for eager execution variables.

There is a complete list of these operations at `https://www.tensorflow.org/api_guides/python/math_ops`.

Casting a tensor to another (tensor) datatype

TensorFlow variables of one type may be cast (coerced) to another type. More details may be found at `https://www.tensorflow.org/api_docs/python/tf/cast`.

Take the following example:

```
i = tf.cast(t1, dtype=tf.int32) # 42
i
```

The output will be as follows:

```
<tf.Tensor: id=116, shape=(), dtype=int32, numpy=42>
```

With truncation, it would be as follows:

```
j = tf.cast(tf.constant(4.9), dtype=tf.int32) # 4
j
```

The output will be as follows:

```
<tf.Tensor: id=119, shape=(), dtype=int32, numpy=4>
```

Declaring ragged tensors

A ragged tensor is a tensor with one or more ragged dimensions. Ragged dimensions are dimensions that have slices that may have different lengths.

There are a variety of methods for declaring ragged arrays, the simplest being a constant ragged array.

The following example shows how to declare a constant ragged array and the lengths of the individual slices:

```
ragged =tf.ragged.constant([[5, 2, 6, 1], [], [4, 10, 7], [8], [6,7]])

print(ragged)
print(ragged[0,:])
print(ragged[1,:])
print(ragged[2,:])
print(ragged[3,:])
print(ragged[4,:])
```

The output is as follows:

```
<tf.RaggedTensor [[5, 2, 6, 1], [], [4, 10, 7], [8], [6, 7]]>
tf.Tensor([5 2 6 1], shape=(4,), dtype=int32)
tf.Tensor([], shape=(0,), dtype=int32)
tf.Tensor([ 4 10  7], shape=(3,), dtype=int32)
tf.Tensor([8], shape=(1,), dtype=int32)
tf.Tensor([6 7], shape=(2,), dtype=int32)
```

Note the shape of the individual slices.

A common way of creating a ragged array is by using the tf.RaggedTensor.from_row_splits() method, which has the following signature:

```
@classmethod
from_row_splits(
    cls,
```

```
      values,
      row_splits,
      name=None
)
```

Here, `values` is a list of the values to be turned into the ragged array, and `row_splits` is a list of the positions where the value list is to be split, so that the values for row `ragged[i]` are stored in `ragged.values[ragged.row_splits[i]:ragged.row_splits[i+1]]`:

```
print(tf.RaggedTensor.from_row_splits(values=[5, 2, 6, 1, 4, 10, 7, 8, 6, 7],
row_splits=[0, 4, 4, 7, 8, 10]))
```

`RaggedTensor` is as follows:

```
<tf.RaggedTensor [[5, 2, 6, 1], [], [4, 10, 7], [8], [6, 7]]>
```

Providing useful TensorFlow operations

There is a complete list of all TensorFlow Python modules, classes, and functions at `https://www.tensorflow.org/api_docs/python/tf`.

All of the maths functions can be found at `https://www.tensorflow.org/api_docs/python/tf/math`.

In this section, we will look at some useful TensorFlow operations, especially within the context of neural network programming.

Finding the squared difference between two tensors

Later in this book, we will need to find the square of the difference between two tensors. The method is as follows:

```
tf.math.squared.difference( x,  y, name=None)
```

Take the following example:

```
x = [1,3,5,7,11]
y = 5
s = tf.math.squared_difference(x,y)
s
```

The output will be as follows:

```
<tf.Tensor: id=279, shape=(5,), dtype=int32, numpy=array([16, 4, 0, 4, 36],
dtype=int32)>
```

Note that the Python variables, x and y, are cast into tensors and that y is then broadcast across x in this example. So, for example, the first calculation is $(1-5)^2 = 16$.

Finding a mean

The following is the signature of tf.reduce_mean().

Note that, in what follows, all TensorFlow operations have a name argument that can safely be left to the default of None when using eager execution as its purpose is to identify the operation in a computational graph.

Note that this is equivalent to np.mean, except that it infers the return datatype from the input tensor, whereas np.mean allows you to specify the output type (defaulting to float64):

```
tf.reduce_mean(input_tensor, axis=None, keepdims=None, name=None)
```

It is frequently necessary to find the mean value of a tensor. When this is done across a single axis, this axis is said to be reduced.

Here are some examples:

```
numbers = tf.constant([[4., 5.], [7., 3.]])
```

Finding the mean across all axes

Find the mean across all axes (that is, use the default axis = None) with this:

```
tf.reduce_mean(input_tensor=numbers)
#( 4. + 5. + 7. + 3.)/4 = 4.75
```

The output will be as follows:

```
<tf.Tensor: id=272, shape=(), dtype=float32, numpy=4.75>
```

Finding the mean across columns

Find the mean across columns (that is, reduce rows) with this:

```
tf.reduce_mean(input_tensor=numbers, axis=0) # [ (4. + 7. )/2 , (5. + 3.)/2
] = [5.5, 4.]
```

The output will be as follows:

```
<tf.Tensor: id=61, shape=(2,), dtype=float32, numpy=array([5.5, 4. ],
dtype=float32)>
```

When `keepdims` is `True`, the reduced axis is retained with a length of 1:

```
tf.reduce_mean(input_tensor=numbers, axis=0, keepdims=True)
```

The output is as follows:

```
array([[5.5, 4.]])          (1 row, 2 columns)
```

Finding the mean across rows

Find the mean across rows (that is, reduce columns) with this:

```
tf.reduce_mean(input_tensor=numbers, axis=1) # [ (4. + 5. )/2 , (7. + 3.
)/2] = [4.5, 5]
```

The output will be as follows:

```
<tf.Tensor: id=64, shape=(2,), dtype=float32, numpy=array([4.5, 5. ],
dtype=float32)>
```

When `keepdims` is `True`, the reduced axis is retained with a length of 1:

```
tf.reduce_mean(input_tensor=numbers, axis=1, keepdims=True)
```

The output is as follows:

```
([[4.5], [5]])          (2 rows, 1 column)
```

Generating tensors filled with random values

Random values are frequently required when developing neural networks, for example, when initializing weights and biases. TensorFlow provides a number of methods for generating these random values.

Using tf.random.normal()

`tf.random.normal()` outputs a tensor of the given shape filled with values of the `dtype` type from a normal distribution.

The required signature is as follows:

```
tf. random.normal(shape, mean = 0, stddev =2, dtype=tf.float32, seed=None,
name=None)
```

Take this, for example:

```
tf.random.normal(shape = (3,2), mean=10, stddev=2, dtype=tf.float32,
seed=None,  name=None)
ran = tf.random.normal(shape = (3,2), mean=10.0, stddev=2.0)
print(ran)
```

The output will be as follows:

```
<tf.Tensor: id=13, shape=(3, 2), dtype=float32, numpy= array([[ 8.537131 ,
7.6625767], [10.925293 , 11.804686 ], [ 9.3763075, 6.701221 ]],
dtype=float32)>
```

Using tf.random.uniform()

The required signature is this:

```
tf.random.uniform(shape, minval = 0, maxval= None, dtype=tf.float32,
seed=None,  name=None)
```

This outputs a tensor of the given shape filled with values from a uniform distribution in the range `minval` to `maxval`, where the lower bound is inclusive but the upper bound isn't.

Take this, for example:

```
tf.random.uniform(shape = (2,4),  minval=0, maxval=None, dtype=tf.float32,
seed=None,  name=None)
```

The output will be as follows:

```
tf.Tensor( [[ 6 7] [ 0 12]], shape=(2, 2), dtype=int32)
```

Note that, for both of these random operations, if you want the random values generated to be repeatable, then use `tf.random.set_seed()`. Use of a non-default datatype is also shown here:

```
tf.random.set_seed(11)
ran1 = tf.random.uniform(shape = (2,2), maxval=10, dtype = tf.int32)
ran2 =  tf.random.uniform(shape = (2,2), maxval=10, dtype = tf.int32)
print(ran1) #Call 1
print(ran2)

tf.random.set_seed(11) #same seed
ran1 = tf.random.uniform(shape = (2,2), maxval=10, dtype = tf.int32)
ran2 = tf.random.uniform(shape = (2,2), maxval=10, dtype = tf.int32)
print(ran1) #Call 2
print(ran2)
```

`Call 1` and `Call 2` will return the same set of values.

The output will be as follows:

```
tf.Tensor(
[[4 6]
 [5 2]], shape=(2, 2), dtype=int32)
tf.Tensor(
[[9 7]
 [9 4]], shape=(2, 2), dtype=int32)

tf.Tensor(
[[4 6]
 [5 2]], shape=(2, 2), dtype=int32)
tf.Tensor(
[[9 7]
 [9 4]], shape=(2, 2), dtype=int32)
```

Using a practical example of random values

Here is a little example adapted for eager execution from `https://colab.research.google.com/notebooks/mlcc/creating_and_manipulating_tensors.ipynb#scrollTo=6UUluecQSCvr`.

Notice that this example shows how to initialize an eager variable with a call to a TensorFlow function.

```
dice1 = tf.Variable(tf.random.uniform([10, 1], minval=1, maxval=7,
dtype=tf.int32))
  dice2 = tf.Variable(tf.random.uniform([10, 1], minval=1, maxval=7,
```

```
dtype=tf.int32))

    # We may add dice1 and dice2 since they share the same shape and size.
    dice_sum = dice1 + dice2

    # We've got three separate 10x1 matrices. To produce a single
    # 10x3 matrix, we'll concatenate them along dimension 1.
    resulting_matrix = tf.concat(values=[dice1, dice2, dice_sum], axis=1)

    print(resulting_matrix)
```

The sample output will be as follows:

```
tf.Tensor(
[[ 5  4  9]
 [ 5  1  6]
 [ 2  4  6]
 [ 5  6 11]
 [ 4  4  8]
 [ 4  6 10]
 [ 2  2  4]
 [ 5  6 11]
 [ 2  6  8]
 [ 5  4  9]], shape=(10, 3), dtype=int32)
```

Finding the indices of the largest and smallest element

We will now look at how to find the indices of the elements with the largest and smallest values, respectively, across the axes of a tensor.

The signatures of the functions are as follows:

```
tf.argmax(input, axis=None, name=None, output_type=tf.int64 )

tf.argmin(input, axis=None, name=None, output_type=tf.int64 )
```

Take this, for example:

```
# 1-D tensor
t5 = tf.constant([2, 11, 5, 42, 7, 19, -6, -11, 29])
print(t5)
i = tf.argmax(input=t5)
print('index of max; ', i)
print('Max element: ',t5[i].numpy())
```

```
i = tf.argmin(input=t5,axis=0).numpy()
print('index of min: ', i)
print('Min element: ',t5[i].numpy())

t6 = tf.reshape(t5, [3,3])

print(t6)
i = tf.argmax(input=t6,axis=0).numpy() # max arg down rows
print('indices of max down rows; ', i)
i = tf.argmin(input=t6,axis=0).numpy() # min arg down rows
print('indices of min down rows ; ',i)

print(t6)
i = tf.argmax(input=t6,axis=1).numpy() # max arg across cols
print('indices of max across cols: ',i)
i = tf.argmin(input=t6,axis=1).numpy() # min arg across cols
print('indices of min across cols: ',i)
```

The output will be as follows:

```
tf.Tensor([ 2 11 5 42 7 19 -6 -11 29], shape=(9,), dtype=int32)

index of max; tf.Tensor(3, shape=(), dtype=int64)
Max element: 42

index of min: tf.Tensor(7, shape=(), dtype=int64)
Min element: -11

tf.Tensor( [[ 2 11 5] [ 42 7 19] [ -6 -11 29]], shape=(3, 3), dtype=int32)
indices of max down rows; tf.Tensor([1 0 2], shape=(3,), dtype=int64)
indices of min down rows ; tf.Tensor([2 2 0], shape=(3,), dtype=int64)

tf.Tensor( [[ 2 11 5] [ 42 7 19] [ -6 -11 29]], shape=(3, 3), dtype=int32)
indices of max across cols: tf.Tensor([1 0 2], shape=(3,), dtype=int64)
indices of min across cols: tf.Tensor([0 1 1], shape=(3,), dtype=int64)
```

Saving and restoring tensor values using a checkpoint

In order to save and load the values of tensors, here is the best method (see Chapter 2, *Keras, a High-Level API for TensorFlow 2*, for methods to save complete models):

```
variable = tf.Variable([[1,3,5,7],[11,13,17,19]])
checkpoint= tf.train.Checkpoint(var=variable)
save_path = checkpoint.save('./vars')
```

```
variable.assign([[0,0,0,0],[0,0,0,0]])
variable
checkpoint.restore(save_path)
print(variable)
```

The output will be as follows:

```
<tf.Variable 'Variable:0' shape=(2, 4) dtype=int32, numpy= array([[ 1, 3,
5, 7], [11, 13, 17, 19]], dtype=int32)>
```

Using tf.function

`tf.function` is a function that will take a Python function and return a TensorFlow graph. The advantage of this is that graphs can apply optimizations and exploit parallelism in the Python function (`func`). `tf.function` is new to TensorFlow 2.

Its signature is as follows:

```
tf.function(
    func=None,
    input_signature=None,
    autograph=True,
    experimental_autograph_options=None
)
```

An example is as follows:

```
def f1(x, y):
    return tf.reduce_mean(input_tensor=tf.multiply(x ** 2, 5) + y**2)

f2 = tf.function(f1)

x = tf.constant([4., -5.])
y = tf.constant([2., 3.])

# f1 and f2 return the same value, but f2 executes as a TensorFlow graph

assert f1(x,y).numpy() == f2(x,y).numpy()
```

The assert passes, so there is no output.

Summary

In this chapter, we started to become familiar with TensorFlow by looking at a number of snippets of code illustrating some basic operations. We had a look at an overview of the modern TensorFlow ecosystem and how to install TensorFlow. We also examined some housekeeping operations, some eager operations, and a variety of TensorFlow operations that will be useful in the rest of this book. There is an excellent introduction to TensorFlow 2 at `www.youtube.com/watch?v=k5c-vg4rjBw`.

Also check out *Appendix A* for details of a `tf1.12` to `tf2` conversion tool. In the next chapter, we will take a look at Keras, which is a high-level API for TensorFlow 2.

Keras, a High-Level API for TensorFlow 2

In this chapter, we will discuss Keras, which is a high-level API for TensorFlow 2. Keras was developed by François Chollet at Google. Keras has become extremely popular for fast prototyping, for building and training deep learning models, and for research and production. Keras is a very rich API; it supports eager execution and data pipelines, and other features, as we will see.

Keras has been available for TensorFlow since 2017, but its use has been extended and further integrated into TensorFlow with the release of TensorFlow 2.0. TensorFlow 2.0 has embraced Keras as the API of choice for the majority of deep learning development work.

It is possible to import Keras as a standalone module, but in this book, we will concentrate on using Keras from within TensorFlow 2. The module is, thus, `tensorflow.keras`.

In this chapter, we will cover the following topics:

- The adoption and advantages of Keras
- The features of Keras
- The default Keras configuration file
- The Keras backend
- Keras data types
- Keras models
- Keras datasets

The adoption and advantages of Keras

Keras is widely used by industry and research, as shown in the following diagram. The *Power Score* rankings were devised by Jeff Hale, who used 11 data sources across 7 distinct categories to gauge framework usage, interest, and popularity. Then, he weighted and combined the data as shown in this Medium article from September 2018: `https://towardsdatascience.com/deep-learning-framework-power-scores-2018-23607ddf297a`:

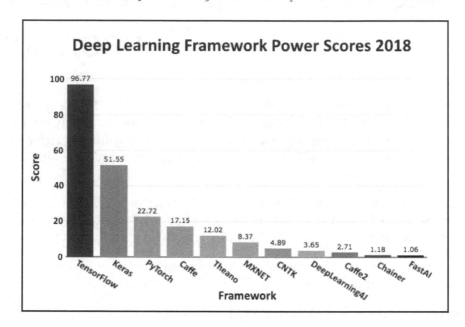

Keras has a number of advantages, including the following:

- It's designed for both new users and experts alike, offering consistent and simple APIs
- It's user friendly with a simple, consistent interface that is optimized for common use cases
- It provides excellent feedback for user errors that is are easily understood and often accompanied by helpful advice
- It's modular and composable; models in Keras are constructed by joining up configurable building blocks
- It's easy to extend by writing custom building blocks
- It is not necessary to import Keras as it is available as `tensorflow.keras`

The features of Keras

If you want to know which version of Keras came with your TensorFlow, use the following command:

```
import tensorflow as tf
print(tf.keras.__version__)
```

At the time of writing, this produced the following (from the alpha build of TensorFlow 2):

```
2.2.4-tf
```

Other features of Keras include built-in support for multi-GPU data parallelism, and also the fact that Keras models can be turned into TensorFlow Estimators and trained on clusters of GPUs on Google Cloud.

Keras is, perhaps, unusual in that it is has a reference implementation maintained as an independent open source project, located at www.keras.io.

It's maintained independently of TensorFlow, although TensorFlow does have a full implementation of Keras in the tf.keras module. The implementation has TensorFlow-specific augmentations, including support for eager execution, by default.

Eager execution means that execution of code is an imperative programming environment, rather than a graph-based environment, which was the only way to work in the initial offering of TensorFlow (prior to v1.5). This imperative (that is, immediate) style allows for intuitive debugging, fast development iteration, support for the TensorFlow SavedModel format, and built-in support for distributed training on CPUs, GPUs, and even Google's own hardware, **Tensor Processing Units** (**TPUs**).

The TensorFlow implementation also has support for tf.data, distribution strategies, exporting models, which can be deployed on mobile and embedded devices via TensorFlow Lite, and feature columns for representing and classifying structured data.

The default Keras configuration file

The default configuration file for Linux users is as follows:

```
$HOME/.keras/keras.json
```

For Windows users, replace `$HOME` with `%USERPROFILE%`.

It is created the first time you use Keras, and may be edited to change the defaults. Here's what that `.json` file contains:

```
{ "image_data_format": "channels_last",
"epsilon": 1e-07,
"floatx": "float32",
"backend": "tensorflow" }
```

The defaults are as follows:

- `image_data_format`: This is a string, either `"channels_last"` or `channels_first`, for the image format. Keras running on top of TensorFlow uses the default.
- `epsilon`: This is a float, being a numeric *fuzzing* constant used to avoid division by zero in some operations.
- `floatx`: This is a string and specifies the default float precision, being one of `"float16"`, `"float32"`, or `"float64"`.
- `backend`: This is a string and specifies the tool that Keras finds itself on top of, being one of `"tensorflow"`, `"theano"`, or `"cntk"`.

There are getter and setter methods, available in `keras.backend`, for all these values; see `https://keras.io/backend/`.

For example, in the following sets, the floating point type for Keras to use is `floatx`, where the `floatx` argument is one of the three precisions shown in the following command:

```
keras.backend.set_floatx(floatx)
```

The Keras backend

Due to its model-level library structure, Keras may have different tensor manipulation engines that handle low-level operations, such as convolutions, tensor products, and the like. These engines are called **backends**. Other backends are available; we will not consider them here.

The same `https://keras.io/backend/` link takes you to a wealth of `keras.backend` functions.

The canonical way to use the Keras `backend` is with the following:

```
from keras import backend as K
```

For example, here is the signature of a useful function:

```
K.constant(value, dtype=None, shape=None, name=None)
```

Here `value` is the value to be given to the constant, `dtype` is the type of the tensor that is created, `shape` is the shape of the tensor that is created, and `name` is an optional name.

An instantiation of this is as follows:

```
from tensorflow.keras import backend as K
const = K.constant([[42,24],[11,99]], dtype=tf.float16, shape=[2,2])
const
```

This produces the following constant tensor. Notice that, because eager execution is enabled, (by default) the value of the constant is given in the output:

```
<tf.Tensor: id=1, shape=(2, 2), dtype=float16, numpy= array([[42., 24.],
[11., 99.]], dtype=float16)>
```

Were eager not to be enabled, the output would be as follows:

```
<tf.Tensor 'Const:0' shape=(2, 2) dtype=float16>
```

Keras data types

Keras **data types** (**dtypes**) are the same as TensorFlow Python data types, as shown in the following table:

Python type	Description
tf.float16	16-bit floating point
tf.float32	32-bit floating point
tf.float64	64-bit floating point
tf.int8	8-bit signed integer
tf.int16	16-bit signed integer
tf.int32	32-bit signed integer
tf.int64	64-bit signed integer
tf.uint8	8-bit unsigned integer
tf.string	Variable-length byte arrays

Python type	Description
tf.bool	Boolean
tf.complex64	Complex number made of two 32-bit floating points—one real and imaginary part
tf.complex128	Complex number made of two 64-bit floating points—one real and one imaginary part
tf.qint8	8-bit signed integer used in quantized Ops
tf.qint32	32-bit signed integer used in quantized Ops
tf.quint8	8-bit unsigned integer used in quantized Ops

Keras models

Keras is based on the concept of a neural network model. The predominant model is called a **Sequence**, being a linear stack of layers. There is also a system using the Keras functional API.

The Keras Sequential model

To build a Keras Sequential model, you *add* layers to it in the same order that you want the computations to be undertaken by the network.

After you have built your model, you *compile* it; this optimizes the computations that are to be undertaken, and is where you allocate the optimizer and the loss function you want your model to use.

The next stage is to *fit* the model to the data. This is commonly known as training the model, and is where all the computations take place. It is possible to present the data to the model either in batches, or all at once.

Next, you evaluate your model to establish its accuracy, loss, and other metrics. Finally, having trained your model, you can use it to make predictions on new data. So, the workflow is: build, compile, fit, evaluate, make predictions.

There are two ways to create a Sequential model. Let's take a look at each of them.

The first way to create a Sequential model

Firstly, you can pass a list of layer instances to the constructor, as in the following example.

We will have much more to say about layers in the next chapter; for now, we will just explain enough to allow you to understand what is happening here.

Acquire the data. `mnist` is a dataset of hand-drawn numerals, each on a 28 x 28 pixel grid. Every individual data point is an unsigned 8-bit integer (`uint8`), as are the labels:

```
mnist = tf.keras.datasets.mnist
(train_x,train_y), (test_x, test_y) = mnist.load_data()
```

The `epochs` variable stores the number of times we are going to present the data to the model:

```
epochs=10
batch_size = 32 # 32 is default in fit method but specify anyway
```

Next, normalize all the data points (x) to be in the float range zero to one, and of the `float32` type. Also, cast the labels (y) to `int64`, as required:

```
train_x, test_x = tf.cast(train_x/255.0, tf.float32), tf.cast(test_x/255.0,
tf.float32)
train_y, test_y = tf.cast(train_y,tf.int64),tf.cast(test_y,tf.int64)
```

The model definition follows.

Notice in the model definition how we are passing a list of layers:

- `Flatten` takes the input of 28 x 28 (that is, 2D) pixel images and produces a 784 (that is, 1D) vector because the next (dense) layer is one-dimensional.
- `Dense` is a fully connected layer, meaning all its neurons are connected to every neuron in the previous and next layers. The following example has 512 neurons, and its inputs are passed through a ReLU (non-linear) activation function.
- `Dropout` randomly turns off a fraction (in this case, 0.2) of neurons in the previous layer. This is done to prevent any particular neuron becoming too specialized and causing *overfitting* of the model to the data, thus impacting on the accuracy metric of the model on the test data (much more on this in later chapters).
- The final `Dense` layer has a special activation function called `softmax`, which assigns probabilities to each of the possible 10 output units:

```
model1 = tf.keras.models.Sequential([
  tf.keras.layers.Flatten(),
  tf.keras.layers.Dense(512,activation=tf.nn.relu),
  tf.keras.layers.Dropout(0.2),
  tf.keras.layers.Dense(10,activation=tf.nn.softmax)
])
```

The `model.summary()` function is a useful eponymous method and gives the following output for our model:

```
Layer (type)                 Output Shape              Param #
=================================================================
flatten_1 (Flatten)          multiple                  0
_____
dense_2 (Dense)              multiple                  401920
_____
dropout_1 (Dropout)          multiple                  0
_____
dense_3 (Dense)              multiple                  5130
=================================================================
Total params: 407,050
Trainable params: 407,050
Non-trainable params: 0
_____
```

The figure of `401920` comes from input = 28 x 28 = 784 x 512 (`dense_2` layer) = giving *784 *512 = 401,408* together with a bias unit for each of the `dense_1` layer neurons, giving *401,408 + 512 = 401,920.*

The figure of `5130` comes in a similar way, from *512* 10 + 10 = 5,130.*

Next, we compile our model, as shown in the following code:

```
optimiser = tf.keras.optimizers.Adam()
model1.compile (optimizer= optimiser,
loss='sparse_categorical_crossentropy', metrics = ['accuracy'])
```

`optimizer` is the method by which the weights of the weighted connections in the model are adjusted to decrease the loss.

`loss` is a measure of the difference between the required output of the model and the actual output, and `metrics` is how we evaluate the model.

To train our model, we use the `fit` method next, shown as follows:

```
model1.fit(train_x, train_y, batch_size=batch_size, epochs=epochs)
```

The output from the call to `fit()` is as follows, showing the epoch training time, the loss, and the accuracy:

```
Epoch 1/10 60000/60000 [==============================] - 5s 77us/step -
loss: 0.2031 - acc: 0.9394
...
Epoch 10/10 60000/60000 [==============================] - 4s 62us/step -
loss: 0.0098 - acc: 0.9967
```

And finally, we can check our trained model for accuracy using the `evaluate` method:

```
model1.evaluate(test_x, test_y)
```

This produces the following output:

```
10000/10000 [==============================] - 0s 39us/step
[0.09151900197149189, 0.9801]
```

This represents a loss of 0.09 and an accuracy of 0.9801 on the test data. An accuracy of 0.98 means that out of 100 test data points, 98 were, on average, correctly identified by the model.

The second way to create a Sequential model

The alternative to passing a list of layers to the `Sequential` model's constructor is to use the `add` method, as follows, for the same architecture:

```
model2 = tf.keras.models.Sequential();
model2.add(tf.keras.layers.Flatten())
model2.add(tf.keras.layers.Dense(512, activation='relu'))
model2.add(tf.keras.layers.Dropout(0.2))
model2.add(tf.keras.layers.Dense(10,activation=tf.nn.softmax))
model2.compile (optimizer= tf.keras.Adam(),
loss='sparse_categorical_crossentropy',
 metrics = ['accuracy'])
```

The `fit()` method performs the training, as we have seen, fitting the inputs to the outputs using the model:

```
model2.fit(train_x, train_y, batch_size=batch_size, epochs=epochs)
```

Then, we evaluate the performance of our model using the `test` data:

```
model2.evaluate(test_x, test_y)
```

This gives us a loss of `0.07` and an accuracy of `0.981`.

Thus, this method of defining a model produces an almost identical result to the first one, as is to be expected, since it is the same architecture, albeit expressed slightly differently, with the same `optimizer` and `loss` functions. Now let's take a look at the functional API.

The Keras functional API

The functional API lets you build much more complex architectures than the simple linear stack of `Sequential` models we have seen previously. It also supports more advanced models. These models include multi-input and multi-output models, models with shared layers, and models with residual connections.

Here is a short example, with an identical architecture to the previous two, of the use of the functional API.

The setup code is the same as previously demonstrated:

```
import tensorflow as tf
mnist = tf.keras.datasets.mnist
(train_x,train_y), (test_x, test_y) = mnist.load_data()
train_x, test_x = train_x/255.0, test_x/255.0
epochs=10
```

Here is the model definition.

Notice how layers are callable on `tensor` and return a tensor as output, and how these input and output tensors are then used to define a model:

```
inputs = tf.keras.Input(shape=(28,28)) # Returns a 'placeholder' tensor
x = tf.keras.layers.Flatten()(inputs)
x = tf.layers.Dense(512, activation='relu',name='d1')(x)
x = tf.keras.layers.Dropout(0.2)(x)
predictions = tf.keras.layers.Dense(10,activation=tf.nn.softmax,
name='d2')(x)

model3 = tf.keras.Model(inputs=inputs, outputs=predictions)
```

Notice how this code produces an identical architecture to that of `model1` and `model2`:

```
model3.summary()

Layer (type)                 Output Shape              Param #
=================================================================
input_3 (InputLayer)         (None, 28, 28)            0
_____
flatten_2 (Flatten)          (None, 784)               0
_____
d1 (Dense)                   (None, 512)               401920
_____
dropout_2 (Dropout)          (None, 512)               0
_____
d2 (Dense)                   (None, 10)                5130
=================================================================
Total params: 407,050
Trainable params: 407,050
Non-trainable params: 0
_____
```

The **None** appears here because we haven't specified how many input items we have (that is, the batch size). It really means *not given*.

The rest of the code is the same as in the previous example:

```
optimiser = tf.keras.optimizers.Adam()
model3.compile (optimizer= optimiser,
loss='sparse_categorical_crossentropy', metrics = ['accuracy'])

model3.fit(train_x, train_y, batch_size=32, epochs=epochs)

model3.evaluate(test_x, test_y)
```

This gives a loss of 0.067 and an accuracy of 0.982, again as expected, for an identical architecture.

Next, let's see how to subclass the Keras model class.

Subclassing the Keras Model class

The Keras Model class may be subclassed as shown in the code that follows. Google states that a *pure* functional style (as in the preceding example) is to be preferred over the subclassing style (we have included it here for completeness, and because it is interesting).

Firstly, notice how the layers are individually declared and named in the constructor (.__init__()).

Then, notice how the layers are chained together in the functional style in the call() method. This method encapsulates what is referred to as the *forward pass*:

```
class MyModel(tf.keras.Model):
 def __init__(self, num_classes=10):
  super(MyModel, self).__init__()
 # Define your layers here.
  inputs = tf.keras.Input(shape=(28,28)) # Returns a placeholder tensor
  self.x0 = tf.keras.layers.Flatten()
  self.x1 = tf.keras.layers.Dense(512, activation='relu',name='d1')
  self.x2 = tf.keras.layers.Dropout(0.2)
  self.predictions = tf.keras.layers.Dense(10,activation=tf.nn.softmax,
name='d2')

 def call(self, inputs):
 # This is where to define your forward pass
 # using the layers previously defined in `__init__`
  x = self.x0(inputs)
```

```
    x = self.x1(x)
    x = self.x2(x)
    return self.predictions(x)

model4 = MyModel()
```

This definition may be used in place of any of the earlier model definitions in this chapter with identical supporting code for data download, and similar code for training/evaluation. This last example is shown in the following code:

```
model4 = MyModel()
batch_size = 32
steps_per_epoch = len(train_x.numpy())//batch_size
print(steps_per_epoch)

model4.compile (optimizer= tf.keras.Adam(),
loss='sparse_categorical_crossentropy',
 metrics = ['accuracy'])

model4.fit(train_x, train_y, batch_size=batch_size, epochs=epochs)

 model4.evaluate(test_x, test_y)
```

The results of this are a loss of 0.068 and accuracy is 0.982; again, virtually identical to the results produced by the other three model-building styles in this chapter.

Using data pipelines

Data may also be passed into the `fit` method as a `tf.data.Dataset()` iterator, using the following code (the data acquisition code is identical to that previously described). The `from_tensor_slices()` method converts the NumPy arrays into a dataset. Notice the `batch()` and `shuffle()` methods chained together. Next, the `map()` method invokes a method on the input images, x, that randomly flips one in two of them across the y-axis, effectively increasing the size of the image set. The labels, y, are left unaltered here. Finally, the `repeat()` method means that the dataset will be re-fed from the beginning when its end is reached (continuously):

```
batch_size = 32
buffer_size = 10000

train_dataset = tf.data.Dataset.from_tensor_slices((train_x,
train_y)).batch(32).shuffle(10000)

train_dataset = train_dataset.map(lambda x, y:
```

```
(tf.image.random_flip_left_right(x), y))
train_dataset = train_dataset.repeat()
```

The code for the `test` set is similar except that no flipping is done:

```
test_dataset = tf.data.Dataset.from_tensor_slices((test_x,
test_y)).batch(batch_size).shuffle(10000)

test_dataset = train_dataset.repeat()
```

Now in the `fit()` function, we can pass the dataset directly in, as follows:

```
steps_per_epoch = len(train_x)//batch_size # required because of the repeat
on the dataset
optimiser = tf.keras.optimizers.Adam()
model5.compile (optimizer= optimiser,
loss='sparse_categorical_crossentropy', metrics = ['accuracy'])
model.fit(train_dataset, batch_size=batch_size, epochs=epochs,
steps_per_epoch=steps_per_epoch)
```

The compile and evaluate code is similar to that previously seen.

The advantages of using `data.Dataset` iterators are that the pipeline takes care of much of the plumbing that normally goes into preparing data, such as batching and shuffling, as we have seen. The various operations can be chained together, as we have also seen.

Saving and loading Keras models

The Keras API in TensorFlow has the ability to save and restore models easily. This is done as follows, and saves the model in the current directory. Of course, a longer path may be passed here:

```
model.save('./model_name.h5')
```

This will save the model architecture, its weights, its training state (`loss`, `optimizer`), and the state of the optimizer, so that you can carry on training the model from where you left off.

Loading a saved model is done as follows. Note that if you have compiled your model, the load will compile your model using the saved training configuration:

```
from tensorflow.keras.models import load_model
new_model = load_model('./model_name.h5')
```

It is also possible to save just the model weights and load them with this (in which case, you must build your architecture to load the weights into):

```
model.save_weights('./model_weights.h5')
```

Then use the following to load it:

```
model.load_weights('./model_weights.h5')
```

Keras datasets

The following datasets are available from within Keras: `boston_housing`, `cifar10`, `cifar100`, `fashion_mnist`, `imdb`, `mnist`, and `reuters`.

They are all accessed with the `load_data()` function. For example, to load the `fashion_mnist` dataset, use the following:

```
(x_train, y_train), (x_test, y_test) =
tf.keras.datasets.fashion_mnist.load_data()
```

Further details may be found at `https://www.tensorflow.org/versions/r2.0/api_docs/python/tf/keras/datasets/`.

Summary

In this chapter, we explored the Keras API with general comments and insights followed by the same basic architecture expressed in four different ways, for training with the `mnist` dataset.

In the next chapter, we will start to use TensorFlow in earnest by exploring a number of supervised learning scenarios, including linear regression, logistic regression, and k-nearest neighbors.

3
ANN Technologies Using TensorFlow 2

In this chapter, we will discuss and exemplify those parts of TensorFlow 2 that are needed for the construction, training, and evaluation of artificial neural networks and their utilization purposes for inference. Initially, we will not present a complete application. Instead, we will focus on individual concepts and techniques before putting them all together and presenting full models in subsequent chapters.

In this chapter, we will cover the following topics:

- Presenting data to an **Artificial Neural Network (ANN)**
- ANN layers
- Gradient calculations for gradient descent algorithms
- Loss functions

Presenting data to an ANN

The canonical way to present data to a TensorFlow ANN, as recommended by Google, is via a data pipeline composed of a `tf.data.Dataset` object and a `tf.data.Iterator` method. A `tf.data.Dataset` object consists of a sequence of elements in which each element contains one or more tensor objects. The `tf.data.Iterator` is a method used to loop over a dataset so that successive individual elements in it may be accessed.

We will look at two important ways of constructing a data pipeline, firstly, from in-memory **NumPy** arrays, and, secondly, from **Comma-Separated Value (CSV)** files. We will also look at a binary TFRecord format.

Using NumPy arrays with datasets

Let's look at some straightforward examples first. Here is a NumPy array:

```
import tensorflow as tf
import numpy as np

num_items = 11
num_list1 = np.arange(num_items)
num_list2 = np.arange(num_items,num_items*2)
```

This is how to create datasets, using the `from_tensor_slices()` method:

```
num_list1_dataset = tf.data.Dataset.from_tensor_slices(num_list1)
```

This is how to create an `iterator` on it using the `make_one_shot_iterator()` method:

```
iterator = tf.compat.v1.data.make_one_shot_iterator(num_list1_dataset)
```

And this is how to use them together, using the `get_next` method:

```
for item in num_list1_dataset:
    num = iterator1.get_next().numpy()
    print(num)
```

 Note that executing this code twice in the same program run will raise an error because we are using a **one-shot** iterator.

It's also possible to access the data in batches with the `batch` method. Note that the first argument is the number of elements to put in each batch and the second is the self-explanatory `drop_remainder` argument:

```
num_list1_dataset = tf.data.Dataset.from_tensor_slices(num_list1).batch(3,
drop_remainder = False)
iterator = tf.compat.v1.data.make_one_shot_iterator(num_list1_dataset)
for item in num_list1_dataset:
    num = iterator.get_next().numpy()
    print(num)
```

There is also a `zip` method, which is useful for presenting features and labels together:

```
dataset1 = [1,2,3,4,5]
dataset2 = ['a','e','i','o','u']
dataset1 = tf.data.Dataset.from_tensor_slices(dataset1)
dataset2 = tf.data.Dataset.from_tensor_slices(dataset2)
zipped_datasets = tf.data.Dataset.zip((dataset1, dataset2))
iterator = tf.compat.v1.data.make_one_shot_iterator(zipped_datasets)
for item in zipped_datasets:
    num = iterator.get_next()
    print(num)
```

We can concatenate two datasets as follows, using the `concatenate` method:

```
ds1 = tf.data.Dataset.from_tensor_slices([1,2,3,5,7,11,13,17])
ds2 = tf.data.Dataset.from_tensor_slices([19,23,29,31,37,41])
ds3 = ds1.concatenate(ds2)
print(ds3)
iterator = tf.compat.v1.data.make_one_shot_iterator(ds3)
for i in range(14):
  num = iterator.get_next()
  print(num)
```

We can also do away with iterators altogether, as shown here:

```
epochs=2
for e in range(epochs):
  for item in ds3:
    print(item)
```

Note that the outer loop here does not raise an error, and so would be the preferred method to use in most circumstances.

Using comma-separated value (CSV) files with datasets

CSV files are a very popular method of storing data. TensorFlow 2 contains flexible methods for dealing with them. The main method here is `tf.data.experimental.CsvDataset`.

CSV example 1

With the following arguments, our dataset will consist of two items taken from each row of the `filename` file, both of the float type, with the first line of the file ignored and columns 1 and 2 used (column numbering is, of course, 0-based):

```
filename = ["./size_1000.csv"]
record_defaults = [tf.float32] * 2 # two required float columns
dataset = tf.data.experimental.CsvDataset(filename, record_defaults,
header=True, select_cols=[1,2])
for item in dataset:
  print(item)
```

CSV example 2

In this example, and with the following arguments, our dataset will consist of one required float, one optional float with a default value of `0.0`, and an `int`, where there is no header in the CSV file and only columns 1, 2, and 3 are imported:

```
#file Chapter_2.ipynb
filename = "mycsvfile.txt"
record_defaults = [tf.float32, tf.constant([0.0], dtype=tf.float32),
tf.int32,]
dataset = tf.data.experimental.CsvDataset(filename, record_defaults,
header=False, select_cols=[1,2,3])
for item in dataset:
  print(item)
```

CSV example 3

For our final example, our `dataset` will consist of two required floats and a required string, where the CSV file has a `header` variable:

```
filename = "file1.txt"
record_defaults = [tf.float32, tf.float32, tf.string ,]
dataset = tf.data.experimental.CsvDataset(filename, record_defaults,
header=False)
or item in dataset:
    print(item[0].numpy(), item[1].numpy(),item[2].numpy().decode() )
# decode as string is in binary format.
```

TFRecords

Another popular choice for storing data is the TFRecord format. This is a binary file format. For large files, it is a good choice because binary files take up less disc space, take less time to copy, and can be read very efficiently from the disc. All this can have a significant effect on the efficiency of your data pipeline and, thus, the training time of your model. The format is also optimized in a variety of ways for use with TensorFlow. It is a little complex because data has to be converted into the binary format prior to storage and decoded when read back.

TFRecord example 1

The first example we show here will demonstrate the bare bones of the techniques. (The file is TFRecords.ipynb).

Because a TFRecord file is a sequence of binary strings, its structure must be specified prior to saving so that it can be properly written and subsequently read back. TensorFlow has two structures for this, tf.train.Example and tf.train.SequenceExample. What you have to do is store each sample of your data in one of these structures, then serialize it, and use tf.python_io.TFRecordWriter to save it to disk.

In the following example, the float array, data, is converted to the binary format and then saved to disc. A feature is a dictionary containing the data that is passed to tf.train.Example prior to serialization and saving. A more elaborate example of this is shown in *TFRecord example 2*:

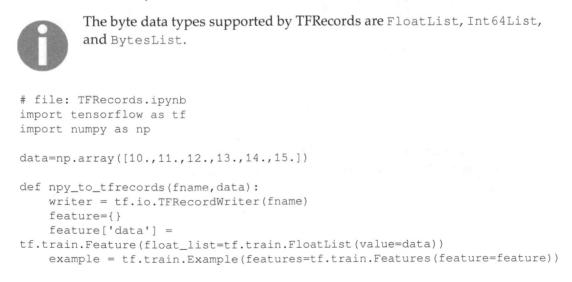 The byte data types supported by TFRecords are FloatList, Int64List, and BytesList.

```
# file: TFRecords.ipynb
import tensorflow as tf
import numpy as np

data=np.array([10.,11.,12.,13.,14.,15.])

def npy_to_tfrecords(fname,data):
    writer = tf.io.TFRecordWriter(fname)
    feature={}
    feature['data'] =
tf.train.Feature(float_list=tf.train.FloatList(value=data))
    example = tf.train.Example(features=tf.train.Features(feature=feature))
```

```
        serialized = example.SerializeToString()
        writer.write(serialized)
        writer.close()

    npy_to_tfrecords("./myfile.tfrecords",data)
```

The code to read the record back is as follows. A `parse_function` function is constructed that decodes the dataset read back from the file. This requires a dictionary (`keys_to_features`) with the same name and structure as the saved data:

```
dataset = tf.data.TFRecordDataset("./myfile.tfrecords")

def parse_function(example_proto):
 keys_to_features = {'data':tf.io.FixedLenSequenceFeature([], dtype =
tf.float32, allow_missing = True) }
    parsed_features = tf.io.parse_single_example(serialized=example_proto,
features=keys_to_features)
    return parsed_features['data']

dataset = dataset.map(parse_function)
iterator = tf.compat.v1.data.make_one_shot_iterator(dataset)
# array is retrieved as one item
item = iterator.get_next()
print(item)
print(item.numpy())
print(item[2].numpy())
```

TFRecord example 2

In this example, we look at a more complicated record structure given by this dictionary:

```
filename = './students.tfrecords'
data = {
        'ID': 61553,
        'Name': ['Jones', 'Felicity'],
        'Scores': [45.6, 97.2]
    }
```

Using this, we can construct a `tf.train.Example` class, again using the `Feature()` method. Note how we have to encode our string:

```
ID = tf.train.Feature(int64_list=tf.train.Int64List(value=[data['ID']]))

Name =
tf.train.Feature(bytes_list=tf.train.BytesList(value=[n.encode('utf-8') for
n in data['Name']]))
```

```
Scores =
tf.train.Feature(float_list=tf.train.FloatList(value=data['Scores']))

example = tf.train.Example(features=tf.train.Features(feature={'ID': ID,
'Name': Name, 'Scores': Scores }))
```

Serializing and writing this record to disc is the same as *TFRecord example 1*:

```
writer = tf.io.TFRecordWriter(filename)
writer.write(example.SerializeToString())
writer.close()
```

To read this back, we just need to construct our `parse_function` function to reflect the structure of the record:

```
dataset = tf.data.TFRecordDataset("./students.tfrecords")

def parse_function(example_proto):
    keys_to_features = {'ID':tf.io.FixedLenFeature([], dtype = tf.int64),
                        'Name':tf.io.VarLenFeature(dtype = tf.string),
                        'Scores':tf.io.VarLenFeature(dtype = tf.float32)
                        }
    parsed_features = tf.io.parse_single_example(serialized=example_proto,
features=keys_to_features)
    return parsed_features["ID"],
parsed_features["Name"],parsed_features["Scores"]
```

The next step is the same as before:

```
dataset = dataset.map(parse_function)

iterator = tf.compat.v1.data.make_one_shot_iterator(dataset)
item = iterator.get_next()
# record is retrieved as one item
print(item)
```

The output is as follows:

```
(<tf.Tensor: id=264, shape=(), dtype=int64, numpy=61553>,
<tensorflow.python.framework.sparse_tensor.SparseTensor object at
0x7f1bfc7567b8>, <tensorflow.python.framework.sparse_tensor.SparseTensor
object at 0x7f1bfc771e80>)
```

Now we can extract our data from `item` (note that the string must be decoded (from bytes) where the default for our Python 3 is `utf8`). Note also that the string and the array of floats are returned as sparse arrays, and to extract them from the record, we use the sparse array `value` method:

```
print("ID: ",item[0].numpy())
name = item[1].values.numpy()
name1= name[0].decode()returned
name2 = name[1].decode('utf8')
print("Name:",name1,",",name2)
print("Scores: ",item[2].values.numpy())
```

One-hot encoding

One-hot encoding (**OHE**) is where a tensor is constructed from the data labels with a 1 in each of the elements corresponding to a label's value, and 0 everywhere else; that is, one of the bits in the tensor is hot (1).

OHE example 1

In this example, we are converting a decimal value of 5 to a one-hot encoded value of 0000100000 using the `tf.one_hot()` method:

```
y = 5
y_train_ohe = tf.one_hot(y, depth=10).numpy()
print(y, "is ",y_train_ohe,"when one-hot encoded with a depth of 10")
# 5 is 00000100000 when one-hot encoded with a depth of 10
```

OHE example 2

This is also nicely shown in the following example using the sample code that imports from the fashion MNIST dataset.

The original labels are integers from 0 to 9, so, for example, a label of 2 becomes 0010000000 when one-hot encoded, but note the difference between the index and the label stored at that index:

```
import tensorflow as tf
from tensorflow.python.keras.datasets import fashion_mnist
tf.enable_eager_execution()
width, height, = 28,28
```

```
n_classes = 10

# load the dataset
(x_train, y_train), (x_test, y_test) = fashion_mnist.load_data()
split = 50000
#split feature training set into training and validation sets
(y_train, y_valid) = y_train[:split], y_train[split:]

# one-hot encode the labels using TensorFlow.
# then convert back to numpy for display
y_train_ohe = tf.one_hot(y_train, depth=n_classes).numpy()
y_valid_ohe = tf.one_hot(y_valid, depth=n_classes).numpy()
y_test_ohe = tf.one_hot(y_test, depth=n_classes).numpy()

# show difference between the original label and a one-hot-encoded label

i=5
print(y_train[i]) # 'ordinary' number value of label at index i=5 is 2
# 2
# note the difference between the index of 5 and the label at that index
which is 2
print(y_train_ohe[i]) #
# 0. 0. 1. 0. 0.0 .0 .0. 0. 0.
```

Next, we will examine the fundamental data structure of a neural network: the **layer** of neurons.

Layers

The fundamental data structure used by ANNs is the **layer**, and many interconnected layers make up a complete ANN. A layer can be envisaged as an array of neurons, although the use of the word *neuron* can be misleading, since there is only a marginal correspondence between human brain neurons and the artificial neurons that make up a layer. Bearing that in mind, we will use the term *neuron* in what follows. As with any computer processing unit, a neuron is characterized by its inputs and its outputs. In general, a neuron has many inputs and one output value. Each input connection carries a weight, w_i.

The following diagram shows a neuron. It is important to note that the activation function, **f**, is non-linear for anything other than trivial ANNs. A general neuron in the network receives inputs from other neurons and each of these carries a weight, $\mathbf{w}_i$, as shown, and the network *learns* by adjusting these weights so that the input generates the required output:

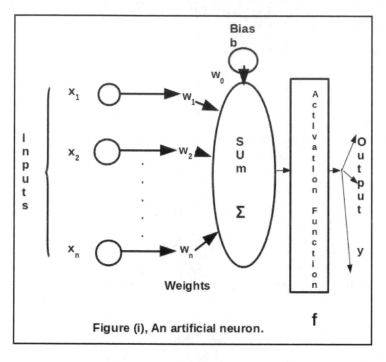

Figure (i), An artificial neuron.

Figure 1: An artificial neuron

The output of a neuron is given by totaling the inputs multiplied by the weights, adding the bias multiplied by its weight, and then applying the activation function (refer to the following diagram).

The following diagram shows how individual artificial neurons and layers are configured to create an ANN:

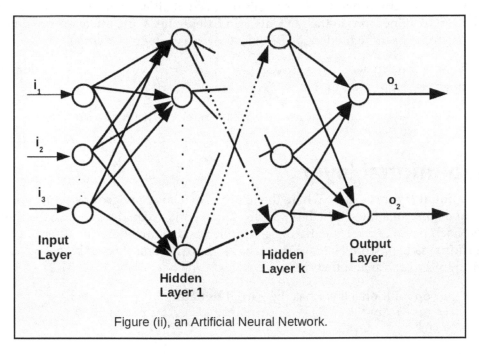

Figure (ii), an Artificial Neural Network.

Figure 2: An artificial neural network

The output of a layer is given by the following formula:

$$output = f(\sum_{1}^{n} W.X + bias)$$

Here, *W* is the weights of the input, *X* is the input vector, and *f* is the non-linear activation function.

There are many types of layers, supporting a large variety of ANN model structures. A very comprehensive list may be found at `https://www.tensorflow.org/api_docs/python/tf/keras/layers`.

Here, we will examine a number of the more popular ones and how TensorFlow implements them.

Dense (fully connected) layer

A **dense layer** is a fully connected layer. This means that all neurons in the previous layer are connected to all neurons in the next layer. In a dense network, all layers are dense. (If a network has three or more hidden layers, it is known as a **deep network**).

A dense layer is constructed by the `layer = tf.keras.layers.Dense(n)` line, where n is the number of output units.

Note that a dense layer is one-dimensional. Please refer to the section on *Models*.

Convolutional layer

A **convolutional layer** is a layer where the neurons in a layer are grouped into small patches by the use of a filter, which is usually square, and created by sliding the filter over the layer. Each patch is *convolved*, that is, multiplied and summed by the filter. **Convolutional nets** or **ConvNets** for short, have proved themselves to be very good at image recognition and manipulation.

For images, a convolutional layer has the partial signature `tf.keras.layers.Conv2D(filters, kernel_size, strides=1, padding='valid')`.

So, in the following example, this first layer has one filter of size (1,1) and its padding is valid. The other padding possibility is *same*.

The difference is that, with the *same* padding, the layer must be padded, often with zeros, around the outside so that after the convolution has taken place, the output size is the same as the layer size. With valid padding, no padding is done and there will be some truncation of the layer if the combination of the stride and the kernel size won't fit exactly on to the layer. The output size is smaller than the layer that is being convolved:

```
seqtial_Net = tf.keras.Sequential([tf.keras.layers.Conv2D(   1, (1, 1),
strides = 1, padding='valid')
```

Max pooling layer

A **max pooling layer** takes the maximum value within its window as the window slides over the layer, in much the same way as a convolution takes place.

The max pooling signature for spatial data, that is, images, is as follows:

```
tf.keras.layers.MaxPooling2D(pool_size=(2, 2), strides=None,
padding='valid', data_format=None)
```

So, to use the defaults, you would simply have the following:

```
layer = tf.keras.maxPooling2D()
```

Batch normalization layer and dropout layer

Batch normalization is a layer that takes its inputs and outputs the same number of outputs with activations that have zero mean and unit variance, as this has been found to be beneficial to learning. Batch normalization regulates the activations so that they neither become vanishingly small nor explosively big, both of which situations prevent the network from learning.

The signature of the `BatchNormalization` layer is as follows:

```
tf.keras.layers.BatchNormalization(axis=-1, momentum=0.99, epsilon=0.001,
center=True, scale=True, beta_initializer='zeros',
gamma_initializer='ones', moving_mean_initializer='zeros',
moving_variance_initializer='ones', beta_regularizer=None,
gamma_regularizer=None, beta_constraint=None, gamma_constraint=None)
```

Hence, to use the defaults, you would simply use the following command:

```
layer = tf.keras.layers.BatchNormalization()
```

Dropout layer is a layer where a certain percentage of the neurons are randomly turned off during training (not during inference). This forces the network to become better at generalizing since individual neurons are discouraged from becoming specialized with respect to their inputs.

The signature of the `Dropout` layer is as follows:

```
tf.keras.layers.Dropout(rate, noise_shape=None, seed=None)
```

The `rate` argument is the fraction of neurons that are turned off.

So, to use this, you would have the following, for example:

```
layer = tf.keras.layers.Dropout(rate = 0.5)
```

Fifty percent of neurons, randomly chosen, would be turned off.

Softmax layer

A **softmax layer** is a layer where the activation of each output unit corresponds to the probability that the output unit matches a given label. The output neuron with the highest activation value is, therefore, the prediction of the net. It is used when the classes being learned are mutually exclusive, so that the probabilities output by the softmax layer total 1.

It is implemented as an activation on a dense layer.

Hence, for example, we have the following:

```
model2.add(tf.keras.layers.Dense(10,activation=tf.nn.softmax))
```

This would add a dense softmax layer with 10 neurons where the activations of the neurons would total 1.

Next, we will talk a little more about activation functions.

Activation functions

It is important to note that neural nets have non-linear activation functions, that is, the functions that are applied to the sum of the weighted inputs to a neuron. Linear activation units are not able to map input layers to output layers in all but trivial neural net models.

There are a number of activation functions in common use, including sigmoid, tanh, ReLU, and leaky ReLU. A good summary, together with diagrams of these functions, may be found here: https://towardsdatascience.com/activation-functions-neural-networks-1cbd9f8d91d6.

Creating the model

There are four methods for creating our ANN model using Keras:

- **Method 1**: Arguments passed to `tf.keras.Sequential`
- **Method 2**: Use of the `.add` method of `tf.keras.Sequential`
- **Method 3**: Use of the Keras functional API
- **Method 4**: By subclassing the `tf.keras.Model` object

Please refer to `Chapter 2`, *Keras, a High-Level API for TensorFlow 2*, for details regarding these four methods.

Gradient calculations for gradient descent algorithms

One of TenorFlow's great strengths is its ability to automatically compute gradients for use in gradient descent algorithms, which, of course, are a vital part of most machine learning models. TensorFlow offers a number of methods for gradient calculations.

There are four ways to automatically compute gradients when eager execution is enabled (they also work in graph mode):

1. `tf.GradientTape`: Context records computations so that you can call `tf.gradient()` to get the gradients of any tensor computed while recording with respect to any trainable variable
2. `tfe.gradients_function()`: Takes a function (say `f()`) and returns a gradient function (say `fg()`) that can compute the gradients of the outputs of `f()` with respect to the parameters of `f()` or a subset of them
3. `tfe.implicit_gradients()`: This is very similar, but `fg()` computes the gradients of the outputs of `f()` with regard to all trainable variables that these outputs depend on
4. `tfe.implicit_value_and_gradients()`: This is almost identical, but `fg()` also returns the output of the function, `f()`

We will look at the most popular of these, tf.GradientTape. Again, within its context, as a calculation takes place, a record (tape) is made of those calculations so that the tape can be replayed with tf.gradient() and the appropriate automatic differentiation is be implemented.

In the following code, when the sum method is calculated, the tape records the calculations within the tf.GradientTape() context so that the automatic differentiation can be found by calling tape.gradient().

Note how lists are used in this example in [weight1_grad] = tape.gradient(sum, [weight1]).

By default, only one call to tape.gradient() may be made:

```
# by default, you can only call tape.gradient once in a GradientTape
context
weight1 = tf.Variable(2.0)
def weighted_sum(x1):
    return weight1 * x1
with tf.GradientTape() as tape:
    sum = weighted_sum(7.)
    [weight1_grad] = tape.gradient(sum, [weight1])
print(weight1_grad.numpy()) # 7 , weight1*x diff w.r.t. weight1 is x, 7.0,
also see below.
```

In this next example, note that the argument, persistent=True, has been passed to tf.GradientTape(). This allows us to call tape.gradient() more than once. Again, we compute a weighted sum inside the tf.GradientTape context and then call tape.gradient() to calculate the derivatives of each term with respect to its weight variable:

```
# if you need to call tape.gradient() more than once
# use GradientTape(persistent=True)
weight1 = tf.Variable(2.0)
weight2 = tf.Variable(3.0)
weight3 = tf.Variable(5.0)

def weighted_sum(x1, x2, x3):
    return weight1*x1 + weight2*x2 + weight3*x3

with tf.GradientTape(persistent=True) as tape:
    sum = weighted_sum(7.,5.,6.)

[weight1_grad] = tape.gradient(sum, [weight1])
[weight2_grad] = tape.gradient(sum, [weight2])
[weight3_grad] = tape.gradient(sum, [weight3])
```

```
print(weight1_grad.numpy())  #7.0
print(weight2_grad.numpy())  #5.0
print(weight3_grad.numpy())  #6.0
```

Next, we will examine loss functions. These are functions that are optimized during the training of a neural network model.

Loss functions

A `loss` function (that is, an error measurement) is a necessary part of the training of an ANN. It is a measure of the extent to which the calculated output of a network during training differs from its required output. By differentiating the `loss` function, we can find a quantity with which to adjust the weights of the connections between the layers so as to make the calculated output of the ANN more closely match the required output.

The simplest `loss` function is the mean squared error:

$$(1/n) \sum_n (y_n - \hat{y}_n)^2$$

Here, y is the actual label value, and $\hat{y}$ is the predicted label value.

Of particular note is the categorical cross-entropy `loss` function, which is given by the following equation:

$$-\sum_n (y_n log(\hat{y}_n) + (1 - y_n)log(1 - \hat{y}_n))$$

This `loss` function is used when only one class is correct out of all the possible ones and so is used when the `softmax` function is used as the output of the final layer of an ANN.

Note that both of these functions differentiate nicely, as required by backpropagation.

Summary

In this chapter, we looked at a number of technologies that support the creation and use of neural networks.

We covered data presentation to an ANN, layers of an ANN, creating the model, gradient calculations for gradient descent algorithms, loss functions, and saving and restoring models. These topics are important precursors to the concepts and techniques that we will encounter in subsequent chapters when we develop neural network models.

Indeed, in the next chapter, we will start to use TensorFlow in earnest by exploring a number of supervised learning scenarios, including linear regression, logistic regression, and k-nearest neighbors.

2
Section 2: Supervised and Unsupervised Learning in TensorFlow 2.00 Alpha

In this section, we will first see a number of applications of TensorFlow in supervised machine learning, to include linear regression, logistic regression, and clustering. We will then look at unsupervised learning, in particular, at autoencoding, as applied to data compression and denoising.

This section contains the following chapters:

- Chapter 4, *Supervised Machine Learning Using TensorFlow 2*
- Chapter 5, *Unsupervised Learning Using Tensorflow 2*

4
Supervised Machine Learning Using TensorFlow 2

In this chapter, we will discuss and exemplify the use of TensorFlow 2 for supervised machine learning problems for the following situations: linear regression, logistic regression, and **k-Nearest Neighbors** (**KNN**).

In this chapter, we will look at the following topics:

- Supervised learning
- Linear regression
- Our first linear regression example
- The Boston housing dataset
- Logistic regression (classification)
- **k-Nearest Neighbors** (**KNN**)

Supervised learning

Supervised learning is the machine learning scenario in which one or more data points from a set of data points is/are associated with a label. The model then *learns* to predict the labels for unseen data points. For our purposes, each data point will normally be a tensor and will be associated with a label. Supervised learning problems abound in computer vision; for example, an algorithm is shown many pictures of ripe and unripe tomatoes, together with a categorical label indicating whether or not they are ripe, and when the training has concluded, the model is able to predict the status of tomatoes that weren't in its training set. This could have a very direct application in a physical sorting mechanism for tomatoes; or an algorithm that could learn to predict the gender and age of a new face after it has been shown many examples, together with their genders and ages. Furthermore, it could be beneficial if a model could learn to predict the type of a tree from its image, having been trained on many tree images and their type labels.

Linear regression

A linear regression problem is one where you have to predict the value of one *continuous* variable, given the value of one or more other variables (data points); for example, predicting the selling price of a house, given its floor space. You can plot the known features with their associated labels on a simple linear graph in these examples, as in the familiar *x*, *y* scatter plots, and plot a line that best fits the data. This is known as a **line of best fit**. You can then read off the label corresponding to any value of your feature that lies within the *x* range of the plot.

However, linear regression problems may involve several features in which the terminology **multiple** or **multivariate linear regression** is used. In this case, it is not a line that best fits the data, but a plane (two features) or a hyperplane (more than two features). In the house price example, we could add the number of rooms and the length of the garden to the features. There is a famous dataset, known as the Boston housing dataset, that involves 13 features (for more info, see `https://www.kaggle.com/c/ml210-boston`). The regression problem here is to predict the median value of a home in the Boston suburbs, given these 13 features.

 A word on nomenclature: features are also known as predictor variables or independent variables. Labels are also known as response variables or dependent variables.

Our first linear regression example

We will start with a simple, artificial, linear regression problem to set the scene. In this problem, we construct an artificial dataset where we first create, and hence, know, the line to which we are fitting, but then we'll use TensorFlow to find this line.

We do this as follows—after our imports and initialization, we enter a loop. Inside this loop, we calculate the overall loss (defined as the mean squared error over our dataset, *y*, of points). We then take the derivative of this loss with respect to our weights and bias. This produces values that we can use to adjust our weights and bias to lower the loss; this is known as gradient descent. By repeating this loop a number of times (technically called **epochs**), we can lower our loss to the point where it is as low as it can go, and we can use our trained model to make predictions.

First, we import the required modules (recall that eager execution is the default):

```
import tensorflow as tf
import numpy as np
```

Next, we initialize important constants, as follows:

```
n_examples = 1000 # number of training examples
training_steps = 1000 # number of steps we are going to train for
display_step = 100 # after multiples of this, we display the loss
learning_rate = 0.01 # multiplying factor on gradients
m, c = 6, -5 # gradient and y-intercept of our line, edit these for a
different linear problem
```

A function to calculate our predicted y, given `weight` and `bias` (m and c):

```
def train_data(n, m, c):
    x = tf.random.normal([n]) # n values taken from a normal distribution,
    noise = tf.random.normal([n])# n values taken from a normal
distribution
    y = m*x + c + noise # our scatter plot
    return x, y
def prediction(x, weight, bias):
    return weight*x + bias # our predicted (learned) m and c, expression is
like y = m*x + c
```

A function to take the initial, or predicted, weights and biases and calculate the mean-squared loss (deviation) from y:

```
def loss(x, y, weights, biases):
    error = prediction(x, weights, biases) - y # how 'wrong' our predicted
(learned) y is
    squared_error = tf.square(error)
    return tf.reduce_mean(input_tensor=squared_error) # overall mean of
squared error, scalar value.
```

This is where TensorFlow comes into its own. Using a class called `GradientTape()`, we can write a function to calculate the derivatives (gradients) of our loss with respect to our `weights` and `bias`:

```
def grad(x, y, weights, biases):
    with tf.GradientTape() as tape:
        loss_ = loss(x, y, weights, biases)
    return tape.gradient(loss, [weights, bias]) # direction and value of
the gradient of our weights and biases
```

Set up our regressor for the training loop and display the initial loss as follows:

```
x, y = train_data(n_examples,m,c) # our training values x and y
plt.scatter(x,y)
plt.xlabel("x")
plt.ylabel("y")
plt.title("Figure 1: Training Data")
W = tf.Variable(np.random.randn()) # initial, random, value for predicted
weight (m)
B = tf.Variable(np.random.randn()) # initial, random, value for predicted
bias (c)

print("Initial loss: {:.3f}".format(loss(x, y, W, B)))
```

The output is shown as follows:

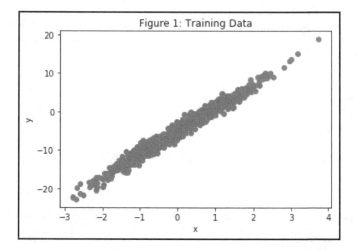

Next, our main training loop. The idea here is to adjust our `weights` and `bias` by small amounts, factored by our `learning_rate`, to successively lower the loss to the points on which we have converged on our line of best fit:

```
for step in range(training_steps): #iterate for each training step
    deltaW, deltaB = grad(x, y, W, B) # direction(sign) and value of the
gradients of our loss
    # with respect to our weights and bias
        change_W = deltaW * learning_rate # adjustment amount for weight
        change_B = deltaB * learning_rate # adjustment amount for bias
        W.assign_sub(change_W) # subract change_W from W
        B.assign_sub(change_B) # subract change_B from B
        if step==0 or step % display_step == 0:
```

```
    # print(deltaW.numpy(), deltaB.numpy()) # uncomment if you want to see
the gradients
    print("Loss at step {:02d}: {:.6f}".format(step, loss(x, y, W, B)))
```

The final results are as follows:

```
print("Final loss: {:.3f}".format(loss(x, y, W, B)))
print("W = {}, B = {}".format(W.numpy(), B.numpy()))
print("Compared with m = {:.3f}, c = {:.3f}".format(m, c)," of the original
line")
xs = np.linspace(-3, 4, 50)
ys = W.numpy()*xs + B.numpy()
plt.scatter(xs,ys)
plt.xlabel("x")
plt.ylabel("y")
plt.title("Figure 2: Line of Best Fit")
```

You should see that the values found for W and B are very close to the values we used for m and c, as is to be expected:

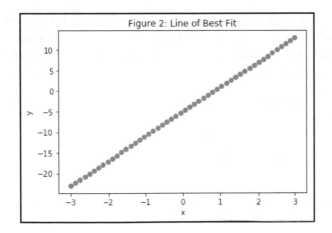

The Boston housing dataset

Next, we will apply a similar regression technique to the Boston housing dataset.

The main difference between this and our previous artificial dataset, which had just one feature, is that the Boston housing dataset is real data and has 13 features. This is a regression problem because house prices—the label—we take as being continuously valued.

Again, we start with our imports, as follows:

```
import tensorflow as tf
from sklearn.datasets import load_boston
from sklearn.preprocessing import scale
import numpy as np
```

And our important constants are shown as follows:

```
learning_rate = 0.01
epochs = 10000
display_epoch = epochs//20
n_train = 300
n_valid = 100
```

Next, we load our dataset and split it into training, validation, and test sets. We train on the training set, and check and fine-tune our trained model on the validation set, to make sure we have no overfitting, for example. Then we use the test set to give a final accuracy measurement, and to see how well our model performs on completely unseen data.

Notice the `scale` method. This is used to convert the data into sets with zero mean and unit standard deviation. The `sklearn.preprocessing` method `scale` achieves this by subtracting the mean from each data point in a feature set, and then dividing each feature by the standard deviation of that set.

This is done because it aids the convergence of our model. All the features are also cast into the `float32` data type:

```
features, prices = load_boston(True)
 n_test = len(features) - n_train - n_valid

# Keep n_train samples for training
 train_features = tf.cast(scale(features[:n_train]), dtype=tf.float32)
 train_prices = prices[:n_train]

# Keep n_valid samples for validation
 valid_features = tf.cast(scale(features[n_train:n_train+n_valid]),
dtype=tf.float32)
 valid_prices = prices[n_train:n_train+n_valid]

# Keep remaining n_test data points as test set)
 test_features =
tf.cast(scale(features[n_train+n_valid:n_train+n_valid+n_test]),
dtype=tf.float32)

test_prices = prices[n_train + n_valid : n_train + n_valid + n_test]
```

Next, we have functions that are similar to those in the last example. Firstly, notice we are now using the more popular route, mean squared error:

```
# A loss function using root mean-squared error
def loss(x, y, weights, bias):
  error = prediction(x, weights, bias) - y # how 'wrong' our predicted
(learned) y is
  squared_error = tf.square(error)
  return tf.sqrt(tf.reduce_mean(input_tensor=squared_error)) # squre root
of overall mean of squared error.
```

Next, we find the direction and value of the gradient of our loss with respect to the weights and bias:

```
# Find the derivative of loss with respect to weight and bias
def gradient(x, y, weights, bias):
  with tf.GradientTape() as tape:
    loss_value = loss(x, y, weights, bias)
  return tape.gradient(loss_value, [weights, bias])# direction and value of
the gradient of our weight and bias
```

Then we interrogate our device, set our initial weights to random values and our bias to 0, and print our initial loss.

Notice that W is now a 13 by 1 vector, as shown here:

```
# Start with random values for W and B on the same batch of data
W = tf.Variable(tf.random.normal([13, 1],mean=0.0, stddev=1.0,
dtype=tf.float32))
B = tf.Variable(tf.zeros(1) , dtype = tf.float32)
print(W,B)
print("Initial loss: {:.3f}".format(loss(train_features, train_prices,W,
B)))
```

Now, on to our main training loop. The idea here is to adjust our weights and bias by small amounts, factored by our learning_rate, to successively lower the loss to the point where we have converged on our line of best fit. As mentioned before, this technique is known as **gradient descent**:

```
for e in range(epochs): #iterate for each training epoch
    deltaW, deltaB = gradient(train_features, train_prices, W, B) #
direction (sign) and value of the gradient of our weight and bias
    change_W = deltaW * learning_rate # adjustment amount for weight
    change_B = deltaB * learning_rate # adjustment amount for bias
    W.assign_sub(change_W) # subract from W
    B.assign_sub(change_B) # subract from B
    if e==0 or e % display_epoch == 0:
```

```
        # print(deltaW.numpy(), deltaB.numpy()) # uncomment if you want to
see the gradients
        print("Validation loss after epoch {:02d}: {:.3f}".format(e,
loss(valid_features, valid_prices, W, B)))
```

Finally, let's compare an actual house price with its prediction, as follows:

```
example_house = 69
y = test_prices[example_house]
y_pred = prediction(test_features,W.numpy(),B.numpy())[example_house]
print("Actual median house value",y," in $10K")
print("Predicted median house value ",y_pred.numpy()," in $10K")
```

Logistic regression (classification)

This type of problem is confusingly named because regression, as we have seen, implies a continuously valued label, such as the median price of a house, or the height of a tree.

This is not the case with logistic regression. When you have a problem requiring logistic regression, it means that the label is `categorical`; for example, zero or one, `True` or `False`, yes or no, cat or dog, or it may more than two categorical values; for example, red, blue or, green, or one, two, three, four, or five, or the type of a given flower. The labels normally have probabilities associated with them; for example, P(cat=0.92), P(dog=0.08). Thus, logistic regression is also known as **classification**.

In our next example, we will use logistic regression to predict the category of items of fashion using the `fashion_mnist` dataset.

Here are a few examples:

Logistic regression to predict the category of items

We can train our model on 50,000 images, validate on 10,000 images, and test on a further 10,000 images.

First, we import the modules required for setting up our initial model and training it, and enable eager execution:

```
import numpy as np
import tensorflow as tf
import keras
from tensorflow.python.keras.datasets import fashion_mnist #this is our
dataset
from keras.callbacks import ModelCheckpoint

tf.enable_eager_execution()
```

Next, we initialize our important constants, as follows:

```
# important constants
batch_size = 128
epochs = 20
n_classes = 10
learning_rate = 0.1
width = 28 # of our images
height = 28 # of our images
```

Then, we associate the indices of our fashion labels (which we train on) with their labels, so we can print out our results pictorially later:

```
fashion_labels =

["Shirt/top","Trousers","Pullover","Dress","Coat","Sandal","Shirt","Sneaker
","Bag","Ankle boot"]
 #indices 0        1        2        3        4        5        6        7
8        9

# Next, we load our fashion data set,
# load the dataset
 (x_train, y_train), (x_test, y_test) = fashion_mnist.load_data()
```

Then, we convert each integer-valued pixel in each of our images to float32 and divide by 255 to normalize them:

```
# normalize the features for better training
 x_train = x_train.astype('float32') / 255.
 x_test = x_test.astype('float32') / 255.
```

x_train now consists of 60000, float32 values, and x_test holds 10000 similar values.

Then, we flatten the feature set, ready for training:

```
# flatten the feature set for use by the training algorithm
 x_train = x_train.reshape((60000, width * height))
 x_test = x_test.reshape((10000, width * height))
```

Then, we further split our training sets, x_train, and y_train, into the training and validation sets:

```
split = 50000
 #split training sets into training and validation sets
 (x_train, x_valid) = x_train[:split], x_train[split:]
 (y_train, y_valid) = y_train[:split], y_train[split:]
```

Many machine learning algorithms work best if the labels are one-hot encoded, so we do this next. But note that we are converting the one-hot tensors produced back to (one-hot) NumPy arrays, ready for use by Keras later:

```
# one hot encode the labels using TensorFLow.
 # then convert back to numpy as we cannot combine numpy
 # and tensors as input to keras later
 y_train_ohe = tf.one_hot(y_train, depth=n_classes).numpy()
 y_valid_ohe = tf.one_hot(y_valid, depth=n_classes).numpy()
 y_test_ohe = tf.one_hot(y_test, depth=n_classes).numpy()
 #or use tf.keras.utils.to_categorical(y_train,10)
```

Here is a snippet of code that shows a value in the range of zero to nine, together with its one-hot encoded version:

```
# show difference between original label and one-hot-encoded label
 i=5
 print(y_train[i]) # 'ordinairy' number value of label at index i
 print (tf.one_hot(y_train[i], depth=n_classes))# same value as a 1. in
 correct position in an length 10 1D tensor
 print(y_train_ohe[i]) # same value as a 1. in correct position in an length
 10 1D numpy array
```

It's important here to notice the difference between the index i, and the label stored at index i. Here is another snippet of code to show the first 10 items of fashion from y_train:

```
# print sample fashion images.
 # we have to reshape the image held in x_train back to width by height
 # as we flattened it for training into width*height
 import matplotlib.pyplot as plt
 %matplotlib inline
 _, image = plt.subplots(1,10,figsize=(8,1))

 for i in range(10):
```

```
image[i].imshow(np.reshape(x_train[i],(width, height)), cmap="Greys")
print(fashion_labels[y_train[i]],sep='', end='')
```

Now we get to an important and generalizable part of the code. Google recommends that, for creating any type of machine learning model, the model is created by subclassing `tf.keras.Model`.

This has the immediate advantage that all the functionality of `tf.keras.Model` is available to us in our subclassed model, including compiling and training routines, and layer functionality, about which we will have much more to say in subsequent chapters.

For our logistic regression example, we need to write two methods in our subclass. Firstly, we need to write a constructor, which calls the constructor of our superclass, so that our model is created correctly. Here, we pass in the number of classes that we are using (10), and use this constructor when a model is instantiated to create a single layer. We must also declare the `call` method, and use this to program what happens during the forward pass of our model's training.

We will be saying much more about this scenario later, when we consider neural networks that have a forward and a backward pass. For our present purposes, we just need to know that in the call method, we take `softmax` of the input to produce the output. What the `softmax` function does is to take a vector (or a tensor) and, at the position whose element has the maximum value for the vector, overwrite this with a value that is almost one, and at all other positions, overwrite with a value that is almost zero. This is very similar to what one-hot encoding does. Notice in this method that, since `softmax` is not implemented for a GPU, we must force execution on the CPU:

```
# model definition (the canonical Google way)
class LogisticRegression(tf.keras.Model):

    def __init__(self, num_classes):
        super(LogisticRegression, self).__init__() # call the constructor
of the parent class (Model)
        self.dense = tf.keras.layers.Dense(num_classes) #create an empty
layer called dense with 10 elements.

    def call(self, inputs, training=None, mask=None): # required for our
forward pass
        output = self.dense(inputs) # copy training inputs into our layer

        # softmax op does not exist on the gpu, so force execution on the
CPU
        with tf.device('/cpu:0'):
            output = tf.nn.softmax(output) # softmax is near one for
maximum value in output
```

```
                                           # and near zero for the other
    values.

        return output
```

We are now ready to compile and train our model.

First, we decide which device is available, and use it. We then declare our model using the class we developed. After declaring the optimizer we are going to use, we compile our model. The loss we are using, categorical cross entropy (also known as **log loss**), is normally used for logistic regression because of the requirement that the predictions are probabilities.

The optimizer is a matter of choice and efficacy, there are a number available (see `https://www.tensorflow.org/api_guides/python/train#Optimizers`). The `model.compile` call, with its three arguments, is next. It prepares our model for training, as we shall see shortly.

At the time of writing, the choice of optimizers is limited; `categorical_crossentropy` is the normal loss function for multiple label logistic regression problems and the `'accuracy'` metric is the metric normally used for classification problems.

Note that next, we have to make a dummy call to the `model.call` method with a sample size of just one of our input images, otherwise the `model.fit` call will try to load the whole dataset in memory to determine the input feature size.

Next, we establish a `ModelCheckpoint` instance, which is used to save our best model during training, and then we train our model using the `model.fit` call.

The easiest way to find out about all the different arguments to `model.compile` and `model.fit` (and all other Python or TensorFlow classes or methods) is to work in a Jupyter Notebook and press *Shift + Tab + Tab* whilst your cursor is sitting on the class or method call in question.

As you can see from the code, `model.fit` saves the best model, using a `callbacks` method, (as determined by validation accuracy) as it trains, and we then load the best model. Finally, we evaluate our model on our test set, as follows:

```
    # build the model
    model = LogisticRegression(n_classes)
    # compile the model
    #optimiser = tf.train.GradientDescentOptimizer(learning_rate)
    optimiser =tf.keras.optimizers.Adam() #not supported in eager execution
    mode.
    model.compile(optimizer=optimiser, loss='categorical_crossentropy',
    metrics=['accuracy'], )
```

```
# TF Keras tries to use the entire dataset to determine the shape without
this step when using .fit()
# So, use one sample of the provided input dataset size to determine
input/output shapes for the model
dummy_x = tf.zeros((1, width * height))
model.call(dummy_x)


checkpointer = ModelCheckpoint(filepath="./model.weights.best.hdf5",
verbose=2, save_best_only=True, save_weights_only=True)
    # train the model
model.fit(x_train, y_train_ohe, batch_size=batch_size, epochs=epochs,
            validation_data=(x_valid, y_valid_ohe),
callbacks=[checkpointer], verbose=2)
    #load model with the best validation accuracy
model.load_weights("./model.weights.best.hdf5")

    # evaluate the model on the test set
scores = model.evaluate(x_test, y_test_ohe, batch_size, verbose=2)
print("Final test loss and accuracy :", scores)
y_predictions = model.predict(x_test)
```

Finally, for our logistic regression example, we have some code to check one test item of fashion to see if its prediction is accurate:

```
    # example of one predicted versus one true fashion label
index = 42
index_predicted = np.argmax(y_predictions[index]) # largest label
probability
index_true = np.argmax(y_test_ohe[index]) # pick out index of element with
a 1 in it
print("When prediction is ",index_predicted)
print("ie. predicted label is", fashion_labels[index_predicted])
print("True label is ",fashion_labels[index_true])


print ("\n\nPredicted V (True) fashion labels, green is correct, red is
wrong")
size = 12 # i.e. 12 random numbers chosen out of x_test.shape[0] =1000, we
do not replace them
fig = plt.figure(figsize=(15,3))
rows = 3
cols = 4
```

Check a random sample of 12 predictions, as follows:

```
for i, index in enumerate(np.random.choice(x_test.shape[0], size = size,
replace = False)):
        axis = fig.add_subplot(rows,cols,i+1, xticks=[], yticks=[]) #
position i+1 in grid with rows rows and cols columns
        axis.imshow(x_test[index].reshape(width,height), cmap="Greys")
        index_predicted = np.argmax(y_predictions[index])
        index_true = np.argmax(y_test_ohe[index])
        axis.set_title(("{}
({})").format(fashion_labels[index_predicted],fashion_labels[index_true]),
                                            color=("green" if
index_predicted==index_true else "red"))
```

True versus (predicted) fashion labels are shown in the following screenshot:

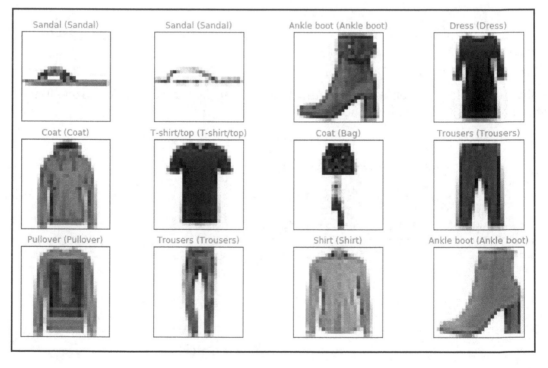

Fashion labels

That concludes our look at logistic regression. We will now look at another very powerful supervised learning technique, k-Nearest Neighbors.

k-Nearest Neighbors (KNN)

The idea behind KNN is relatively straightforward. Given the value of a new particular data point, look at the KNN to the point, and assign a label to the point, depending on the labels of those k neighbors, where *k* is a parameter of the algorithm.

There is no model as such constructed in this scenario; the algorithm merely looks at all the distances between our new point and all the other data points in the dataset, and in what follows, we are going to make use of a famous dataset that consists of three types of iris flowers: `iris setosa`, `iris virginica`, and `iris versicolor`. For each of these labels, the features are petal length, petal width, sepal length, and sepal width. For diagrams showing this dataset, see `https://en.wikipedia.org/wiki/Iris_flower_data_set#/media/File:Iris_dataset_scatterplot.svg`.

There are 150 data points (each consisting of the four measurements noted previously), and 150 associated labels. We will split these into 120 training data points and 30 test data points.

Firstly, we have our usual imports, as follows:

```
import numpy as np
from sklearn import datasets
import tensorflow as tf
# and we next load our data:

iris = datasets.load_iris()
x = np.array([i for i in iris.data])
y = np.array(iris.target)

x.shape, y.shape
```

And we put our flower labels in a list for use later, as shown here:

```
flower_labels = ["iris setosa", "iris virginica", "iris versicolor"]
```

Now it's time to one-hot encode our labels. The `np.eye` returns a two-dimensional array with ones on a diagonal, defaulting to the main diagonal. Indexing with `y` then gives us the required one-hot encoding of `y`:

```
#one hot encoding, another method
y = np.eye(len(set(y)))[y]
y[0:10]
```

Next, we normalize our features to be in the range of zero to one, as shown here:

```
x = (x - x.min(axis=0)) / (x.max(axis=0) - x.min(axis=0))
```

We must work with a randomized set of training features for the algorithm to work properly; we do this next, and also set up our test indices by removing the training indices from the complete range of the dataset:

```
# create indices for the train-test split
np.random.seed(42)
split = 0.8 # this makes 120 train and 30 test features
train_indices = np.random.choice(len(x), round(len(x) * split),
replace=False)
test_indices =np.array(list(set(range(len(x))) - set(train_indices)))
```

We are now in a position to create our training and test features, together with their associated labels:

```
# the train-test split
  train_x = x[train_indices]
  test_x = x[test_indices]
  train_y = y[train_indices]
  test_y = y[test_indices]
```

Now we set our value of k to 5, as follows:

```
k = 5
```

Next, in the Jupyter Notebook, we have our function that predicts the categories of our test data points. We will break this down line by line.

First comes our `distance` function. After this function has been executed, the variable distance contains all the (Manhattan) distances between our 120 training points and the 30 test points; that is, an array of 30 rows by 120 columns—the Manhattan distance, sometimes called the **city block distance**, is the absolute value of the difference between the values of the two data point vectors of x_1 and x_2; that is, $|x_1 - x_2|$. If necessary, as it is in our case, the sum of the individual feature differences is used.

The `tf.expand` adds an extra dimension to `test_x` so that, before the subtraction can take place, both arrays are *enlarged* by broadcasting to make them compatible for the subtraction. Since x is four features, and the `reduce_sum` is over `axis=2`, the result is 30 rows of the distances between our 30 test points and 120 training points. So our `prediction` function is:

```
def prediction(train_x, test_x, train_y,k):
    print(test_x)
```

```
    d0 = tf.expand_dims(test_x, axis =1)
    d1 = tf.subtract(train_x, d0)
    d2 = tf.abs(d1)
    distances = tf.reduce_sum(input_tensor=d2, axis=2)
    print(distances)
    # or
    # distances = tf.reduce_sum(tf.abs(tf.subtract(train_x,
tf.expand_dims(test_x, axis =1))), axis=2)
```

Then we use `tf.nn.top_k` to return, as its second return value, the indices of the KNN. Note that this function's first return value is the values of the distances themselves, which we do not need, hence we "throw them away" (with the underscore):

```
    _, top_k_indices = tf.nn.top_k(tf.negative(distances), k=k)
```

Next, we `gather`, that is, find and return all the training labels associated with the indices of our nearest neighbors, using the indices as slices:

```
    top_k_labels = tf.gather(train_y, top_k_indices)
```

After this we sum the predictions, as follows:

```
    predictions_sum = tf.reduce_sum(input_tensor=top_k_labels, axis=1)
```

Finally, we return the predicted labels by finding the index of the maximum:

```
    pred = tf.argmax(input=predictions_sum, axis=1)
```

Return the resulting prediction, `pred`. For reference, here is a complete function:

```
def prediction(train_x, test_x, train_y,k):
    distances = tf.reduce_sum(tf.abs(tf.subtract(train_x,
tf.cxpand_dims(test_x, axis =1))), axis=2)
    _, top_k_indices = tf.nn.top_k(tf.negative(distances), k=k)
    top_k_labels = tf.gather(train_y, top_k_indices)
    predictions_sum = tf.reduce_sum(top_k_labels, axis=1)
    pred = tf.argmax(predictions_sum, axis=1)
    return pred
```

It can be very instructive to print the shapes of the various tensors as they arise in this function.

The final section of code is straightforward. We zip (concatenate) the predictions of our flower labels with the actual labels, so we can then iterate through them, printing them out and totaling for correctness, and then print the accuracy as a percentage of the number of data points in our test set:

```
i, total = 0 , 0
results = zip(prediction(train_x, test_x, train_y,k), test_y) #concatenate
predicted label with actual label
print("Predicted Actual")
print("--------- ------")
for pred, actual in results:
    print(i,
flower_labels[pred.numpy()],"\t",flower_labels[np.argmax(actual)] )
    if pred.numpy() == np.argmax(actual):
        total += 1
    i += 1
accuracy = round(total/len(test_x),3)*100
print("Accuracy = ",accuracy,"%")
```

If you enter the code yourself, or run the supplied Notebook, you will see that the accuracy is 96.7%, with just one `iris versicolor` misclassified as `iris virginica` (at test index 25).

Summary

In this chapter, we have seen examples of the use of TensorFlow for two situations involving linear regression; where features are mapped to known labels that have continuous values, thus allowing predictions on unseen features to be made. We have also seen an example of logistic regression, better described as classification, where features are mapped to categorical labels, again allowing predictions on unseen features to be made. Finally, we looked at the KNN algorithm for classification.

We will now move on, in `Chapter 5`, *Unsupervised Learning Using TensorFlow 2*, to unsupervised learning, where there is no initial mapping between features and labels, and the task of TensorFlow is to discover relationships between the features.

5

Unsupervised Learning Using TensorFlow 2

In this chapter, we will investigate unsupervised learning using TensorFlow 2. The object of unsupervised learning is to find patterns or relationships in data in which the data points have not been previously labeled; hence, we have only features. This contrasts with supervised learning, where we are supplied with both features and their labels, and we want to predict the labels of new, previously unseen features. In unsupervised learning, we want to find out whether there is an underlying structure to our data. For example, can it be grouped or organized in any way without any prior knowledge of its structure? This is known as **clustering**. For example, Amazon uses unsupervised learning in its recommendation system to make suggestions as to what you might like to buy in the way of books, say, by identifying genre clusters in your previous purchases.

Another use of unsupervised learning is in data compression techniques, where patterns in data can be represented in less memory, without compromising the structure or integrity of the data. In this chapter, we will look at two autoencoders and how they can be used to compress data and how to remove noise from images.

In this chapter, we will deep dive into autoencoders.

Autoencoders

Autoencoding is a data compression and decompression algorithm implemented with an ANN. Since it is an unsupervised form of a learning algorithm, we know that only unlabeled data is required. The way it works is we generate a compressed version of the input by forcing it through a bottleneck, that is, a layer or layers that are less wide than the original input. To reconstruct the input, that is, decompress, we reverse the process. We use backpropagation to both create the representation of the input in the intermediate layer(s), and recreate the input as the output from the representation.

Autoencoding is lossy, that is, the decompressed output will be degraded in comparison to the original input. This is a similar situation to the MP3 and JPEG compression formats.

Autoencoding is data-specific, that is, only data that is similar to that which they have been trained on is properly compressible. For example, an autoencoder trained on pictures of cars would perform badly on pictures of street signs, due to the fact that the features it learned would be unique to cars.

A simple autoencoder

Let's code up a very simple autoencoder that uses an ANN with just one layer. First, as usual, let's start with our imports, as follows:

```
from tensorflow.keras.layers import Input, Dense
from tensorflow.keras.models import Model
from tensorflow.keras.datasets import fashion_mnist
from tensorflow.keras.callbacks import ModelCheckpoint, EarlyStopping
from tensorflow.keras import regularizers

import numpy as np
import matplotlib.pyplot as plt

%matplotlib inline
```

Preprocessing the data

Then, we load the data. For this application, we will use the `fashion_mnist` dataset, which was designed as a drop-in replacement for the famous MNIST dataset. There are examples of these images toward the end of this section. Each data item (pixel in the image) is an unsigned integer in the range 0 to 255, so we first convert it into `float32`, and then scale it into the range zero to one to make it amenable to the learning process later:

```
(x_train, _), (x_test, _) = fashion_mnist.load_data() # we don't need the
labels
x_train = x_train.astype('float32') / 255. # normalize
x_test = x_test.astype('float32') / 255.

print(x_train.shape) # shape of input
print(x_test.shape)
```

This gives shapes, as shown in the following code:

```
(60000, 28, 28)
(10000, 28, 28)
```

Next, we flatten the images since we are going to feed them to a dense layer, which is one-dimensional:

```
x_train = x_train.reshape(( x_train.shape[0], np.prod(x_train.shape[1:])))
#flatten
x_test = x_test.reshape((x_test.shape[0], np.prod(x_test.shape[1:])))

print(x_train.shape)
print(x_test.shape)
```

The shapes are now as follows:

```
(60000, 784)
(10000, 784)
```

Assign the required dimensions, as shown in the following code:

```
image_dim = 784 # this is the size of our input image, 784
encoding_dim = 32 # this is the length of our encoded items.Compression of
factor=784/32=24.5
```

Next, we construct the one-layer encoder and autoencoder models, as follows:

```
input_image = Input(shape=(image_dim, )) # the input placeholder

encoded_image = Dense(encoding_dim, activation='relu',
 activity_regularizer=regularizers.l1(10e-5))(input_image)# "encoded" is
the encoded representation of the input

encoder = Model(input_image, encoded_image)

decoded_image = Dense(image_dim, activation='sigmoid')(encoded_image)#
"decoded" is the lossy reconstruction of the input

autoencoder = Model(input_image, decoded_image) # this model maps an input
to its reconstruction
```

Then, we construct the decoder model, as follows:

```
encoded_input = Input(shape=(encoding_dim,))# create a placeholder for an
encoded (32-dimensional) input

decoder_layer = autoencoder.layers[-1]# retrieve the last layer of the
autoencoder model

decoder = Model(encoded_input, decoder_layer(encoded_input))# create the
decoder model
```

Next, we can compile our autoencoder. The `binary_crossentropy` loss has been chosen since the data is almost binary, and so, we can minimize the per pixel binary cross entropy:

```
autoencoder.compile(optimizer='adadelta', loss='binary_crossentropy')
```

We can define two useful checkpoints. The first one saves the model after every epoch. If `save_best_only=True`, the latest best model, according to the quantity monitored (validation loss), will not be overwritten.

Its signature is the following:

```
keras.callbacks.ModelCheckpoint(filepath, monitor='val_loss', verbose=0,
save_best_only=False, save_weights_only=False, mode='auto', period=1)
```

We declare it as follows:

```
checkpointer1 = ModelCheckpoint(filepath= 'model.weights.best.hdf5' ,
verbose =2, save_best_only = True)
```

The second checkpoint stops training when the change in the monitor (validation loss) is less than `min_delta`, that is, a change less than `min_delta` counts as no improvement. This must happen for `patience` epochs, after which training is halted. Its signature is as follows:

```
EarlyStopping(monitor='val_loss', min_delta=0, patience=0, verbose=0,
mode='auto', baseline=None)
```

We declare it as follows:

```
checkpointer2 = EarlyStopping(monitor='val_loss', min_delta=0.0005,
patience=2, verbose=2, mode='auto')
```

Training

A training run uses the `.fit` method, for which the signature is the following:

```
autoencoder.fit(x=None, y=None, batch_size=None, epochs=1, verbose=1,
callbacks=None, validation_split=0.0, validation_data=None, shuffle=True,
class_weight=None, sample_weight=None, initial_epoch=0,
steps_per_epoch=None, validation_steps=None, max_queue_size=10, workers=1,
use_multiprocessing=False, **kwargs)
```

A vanilla training run is as follows. Notice how we pass in x_train for both x and y, because we are taking the x input and trying to reproduce it on the output (y=x). Notice the following code:

```
epochs = 50
autoencoder.fit(x_train, x_train, epochs=epochs, batch_size=256, verbose-2,
shuffle=True, validation_data=(x_test, x_test))
```

This is followed by some code to compress and decompress (encode and decode) the test data. Remember that encoder and decoder are both models, so we can call the method. Use the predict method on them to generate their output:

```
encoded_images = encoder.predict(x_test) #compress
decoded_images = decoder.predict(encoded_images) #decompress
```

We can also use the ModelCheckpoint checkpoint, in which case our .fit call is the following:

```
epochs = 50
autoencoder.fit(x_train, x_train, epochs=epochs, batch_size=256, verbose=2,
callbacks=[checkpointer1], shuffle=True, validation_data=(x_test, x_test))
```

We also need to load the saved weights as follows, to get the best model back:

```
autoencoder.load_weights('model.weights.best.hdf5' )
encoded_images = encoder.predict(x_test)
decoded_images = decoder.predict(encoded_images)
```

In a similar way, we can use EarlyStopping, in which case the .fit call is as follows:

```
epochs = 50
autoencoder.fit(x_train, x_train, epochs=epochs, batch_size=256, verbose=2,
callbacks=[checkpointer2], shuffle=True, validation_data=(x_test, x_test))
```

Displaying the results

There follows some code to print some before and after items to the screen. We are using the following code:

```
plt.subplot(nrows, ncols, index, **kwargs)
```

Where the subplot will take the `index` position on a grid with `nrows` rows and `ncols` columns, the `index` position starts at one in the upper-left corner and increases to the right to position the items of fashion:

```python
number_of_items = 12 # how many items we will display
plt.figure(figsize=(20, 4))
for i in range(number_of_items):
    # display items before compression
    graph = plt.subplot(2, number_of_items, i + 1)
    plt.imshow(x_test[i].reshape(28, 28))
    plt.gray()
    graph.get_xaxis().set_visible(False)
    graph.get_yaxis().set_visible(False)

    # display items after decompression
    graph = plt.subplot(2, number_of_items, i + 1 + number_of_items)
    plt.imshow(decoded_images[i].reshape(28, 28))
    plt.gray()
    graph.get_xaxis().set_visible(False)
    graph.get_yaxis().set_visible(False)
plt.show()
```

The results are as follows before compression:

After decompression, the results look like this:

So the lossyness of the compress/decompress is obvious. As a possible sanity check, if we use `encoding_dim = 768` (the same number of hidden layer nodes as input), we get the following result:

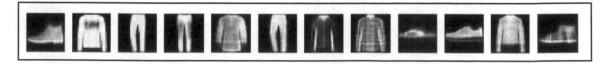

This is perhaps slightly closer to the original. Next, we will look at an application of autoencoding.

An autoencoder application – denoising

A good application of autoencoders is denoising: the process whereby small random artifacts in an image (noise) are removed. We will be replacing our simple one-layer autoencoder with a multi-layer convolutional one.

We will add artificial noise to our fashion items and then remove it. We will also take the opportunity to look at the use of TensorBoard for examining some network training metrics.

Setup

Our initial imports include those for our convolutional network.

Notice that we do not have to Keras explicitly because it is a module of TensorFlow itself, as shown in the following code:

```
from tensorflow.keras.layers import Input, Dense, Conv2D, MaxPooling2D,
UpSampling2D
from tensorflow.keras.models import Model
from tensorflow.keras.datasets import fashion_mnist
from tensorflow.keras.callbacks import TensorBoard
import numpy as np
import matplotlib.pyplot as plt
%matplotlib inline
```

Preprocessing the data

First, load the image data; we don't need the labels as we are only concerned with the images themselves:

```
(train_x, _), (test_x, _) = fashion_mnist.load_data()
```

Next, as before, convert the image data points into float32 value in the range zero to one:

```
train_x = train_x.astype('float32') / 255.
test_x = test_x.astype('float32') / 255.
```

Check the shape, as shown in the following code:

```
print(train_x.shape)
print(test_x.shape)
```

It gives the following result:

```
(60000, 28, 28)
(10000, 28, 28)
```

The input convolutional layer requires the shape given by the following:

```
train_x = np.reshape(train_x, (len(train_x), 28, 28, 1))
test_x = np.reshape(test_x, (len(test_x), 28, 28, 1))
```

Here, the one in the shape is for the grayscale channel; the following is a sanity check on the shape:

```
print(train_x.shape)
print(test_x.shape)
```

This gives the following result:

```
(60000, 28, 28, 1)
(10000, 28, 28, 1)
```

To introduce some random noise into the images, we add an array of `np.random.normal` (that is, Gaussian) values to our training and test sets. The required signature is as follows:

```
numpy.random.normal(loc=0.0, scale=1.0, size=None)
```

Here, `loc` is the center of the distribution, `scale` its standard deviation, and `size` the output shape. So we use the following code:

```
noise = 0.5
train_x_noisy = train_x + noise * np.random.normal(loc=0.0, scale=1.0,
size=train_x.shape)
test_x_noisy = test_x + noise * np.random.normal(loc=0.0, scale=1.0,
size=test_x.shape)
```

Since this may give us values outside the range zero to one, we clip the values to that range:

```
train_x_noisy = np.clip(train_x_noisy, 0., 1.)
test_x_noisy = np.clip(test_x_noisy, 0., 1.)
```

The noisy images

The following code prints a selection of noisy images from the test set. Note how the image has to be reshaped for display:

```
plt.figure(figsize=(20, 2))
for i in range(number_of_items):
    display = plt.subplot(1, number_of_items,i+1)
    plt.imshow(test_x_noisy[i].reshape(28, 28))
    plt.gray()
    display.get_xaxis().set_visible(False)
    display.get_yaxis().set_visible(False)
plt.show()
```

And here are the results, as shown in the following screenshot:

So it's clear that the original images are virtually indistinguishable from the noise.

Creating the encoding layers

Next, we create coding and decoding layers. We will be using the Keras functional API style of setting up the model. We start with a placeholder for the input, in the format required by the (next) convolutional layer:

```
input_image = Input(shape=(28, 28, 1))
```

Next, we have a convolution layer. Recall the signature for the convolutional layer:

```
Conv2D(filters, kernel_size, strides=(1, 1), padding='valid',
data_format=None, dilation_rate=(1, 1), activation=None, use_bias=True,
kernel_initializer='glorot_uniform', bias_initializer='zeros',
kernel_regularizer=None, bias_regularizer=None, activity_regularizer=None,
kernel_constraint=None, bias_constraint=None, **kwargs)
```

We will be using mostly defaults; our first `Conv2D` follows. Notice the kernel size of `(3,3)`; this is the size of the sliding window that Keras applies to the input image. Recall also that `padding='same'` means that the image is padded left and right with zeros, so the input and output layers to the convolution are the size when the kernel (filter) starts with its central "panel" over the first pixel in the image. The default stride of `(1, 1)` means that the sliding window moves one pixel at a time horizontally from the left to the end of the image, then down one pixel, and so on. We will next look at the shape of each layer as follows:

```
im = Conv2D(filters=32, kernel_size=(3, 3), activation='relu',
padding='same')(input_image)
print(x.shape)
```

This gives the following result:

```
(?, 28, 28, 32)
```

? stands for the number of input items.

Next, we have a `MaxPooling2D` layer. Recall that this moves a sliding window over the image, in this case, of a size of `(2, 2)`, and takes the maximum value it finds in each window. Its signature is as follows:

```
MaxPooling2D(pool_size=(2, 2), strides=None, padding='valid',
data_format=None, **kwargs)
```

This is an example of downsampling, because the resultant image is reduced in size. We will use the following code:

```
im = MaxPooling2D((2, 2), padding='same')(im)
print(im.shape)
```

This gives the following result:

```
(?, 14, 14, 32)
```

The rest of the encoding layers are as follows:

```
im = Conv2D(32, (3, 3), activation='relu', padding='same')(im)
print(im.shape)
encoded = MaxPooling2D((2, 2), padding='same')(im)
print(encoded.shape)
```

All of that concludes the encoding.

Creating the decoding layers

To decode, we reverse the process, and use an upsampling layer, UpSampling2D, in place of the max pooling layer. An upsampling layer copies the rows and columns of the data by size [0] and size [1], respectively.

So, in this case, it *undoes* the effect of max pooling layers, albeit with a loss of fine-grainedness. The signature is as follows:

```
UpSampling2D(size=(2, 2), data_format=None, **kwargs)
```

And we use the following:

```
im = UpSampling2D((2, 2))(im)
```

The following are the decoding layers:

```
im = Conv2D(32, (3, 3), activation='relu', padding='same')(encoded)
print(im.shape)
im = UpSampling2D((2, 2))(im)
print(im.shape)
im = Conv2D(32, (3, 3), activation='relu', padding='same')(im)
print(im.shape)
im = UpSampling2D((2, 2))(im)
print(im.shape)
decoded = Conv2D(1, (3, 3), activation='sigmoid', padding='same')(im)
print(decoded.shape)
```

This gives the following result:

```
(?, 7, 7, 32)
(?, 14, 14, 32)
(?, 14, 14, 32)
(?, 28, 28, 32)
(?, 28, 28, 1)
```

So you can see how the decoding layers reverse the process of the encoding layers.

Model summary

Here is a summary of our model:

```
Layer (type)                     Output Shape              Param #
=================================================================
input_1 (InputLayer)             (None, 28, 28, 1)         0

conv2d (Conv2D)                  (None, 28, 28, 32)        320

max_pooling2d (MaxPooling2D)     (None, 14, 14, 32)        0

conv2d_1 (Conv2D)                (None, 14, 14, 32)        9248

max_pooling2d_1 (MaxPooling2     (None, 7, 7, 32)          0

conv2d_2 (Conv2D)                (None, 7, 7, 32)          9248

up_sampling2d (UpSampling2D)     (None, 14, 14, 32)        0

conv2d_3 (Conv2D)                (None, 14, 14, 32)        9248

up_sampling2d_1 (UpSampling2     (None, 28, 28, 32)        0

conv2d_4 (Conv2D)                (None, 28, 28, 1)         289
=================================================================
Total params: 28,353
Trainable params: 28,353
Non-trainable params: 0
```

It's instructive to see how we arrive at the parameter figures.

A formula is a number of parameters = *number of filters x kernel size x depth of the previous layer + number of filters (for the biases)*:

- **input_1**: This is a place holder and has no trainable parameters
- **conv2d**: Number of filters = 32, kernel size = 3*3 = 9, depth of previous layer = 1, so *32*9 + 32 = 320*
- **max_pooling2d**: Max pooling layers have no trainable parameters.
- The **conv2d_1**: Number of filters = 32, kernel size = 3*3 = 9, depth of previous layer = 14 so *32*9*32+ 32 = 9,248*
- **conv_2d_2**, **conv2d_3**: Same as **conv2d_1**
- **conv2d_4**: *1*9*32 +1 = 289*

Model instantiation, compiling, and training

Next, we instantiate our model with its input layer and output layer, and then set the model up for training with the .compile method:

```
autoencoder = Model(inputs=input_img, outputs=decoded)
autoencoder.compile(optimizer='adadelta', loss='binary_crossentropy')
```

Now we are ready to train our model to attempt to recover the images of our fashion items. Notice that we have supplied a call back for TensorBoard, so we can have a look at some training metrics. The Keras TensorBoard signature is as follows:

```
keras.callbacks.TensorBoard(
    ["log_dir='./logs'", 'histogram_freq=0', 'batch_size=32',
'write_graph-True', 'write_grads=False', 'write_images=False',
'embeddings_freq=0', 'embeddings_layer_names=None',
'embeddings_metadata=None', 'embeddings_data=None', "update_freq='epoch'"],
)
```

We will use mostly the defaults, shown as follows:

```
tb = [TensorBoard(log_dir='./tmp/tb', write_graph=True)]
```

Next, we train our autoencoder using the .fit() method. The following code is its signature:

```
fit(x=None, y=None, batch_size=None, epochs=1, verbose=1, callbacks=None,
validation_split=0.0, validation_data=None, shuffle=True,
class_weight=None, sample_weight=None, initial_epoch=0,
steps_per_epoch=None, validation_steps=None, validation_freq=1)
```

Notice how we are using x_train_noisy for the features (input) and x_train for the labels (output):

```
epochs=100
batch_size=128

autoencoder.fit(x_train_noisy, x_train,
epochs=epochs,batch_size=batch_size, shuffle=True,
validation_data=(x_test_noisy, x_test), callbacks=tb)
```

Denoised images

Let's now denoise some noisy images from our test set, by decoding all of the test set in the following first line and then looping over a fixed number (number_of_items) and displaying them. Notice that each image (im) needs to be reshaped prior to displaying it:

```
decoded_images = autoencoder.predict(test_noisy_x)
number_of_items = 10
plt.figure(figsize=(20, 2))
for item in range(number_of_items):
    display = plt.subplot(1, number_of_items,item+1)
    im = decoded_images[item].reshape(28, 28)
  plt.imshow(im, cmap="gray")
    display.get_xaxis().set_visible(False)
    display.get_yaxis().set_visible(False)
plt.show()
```

And we get the following results:

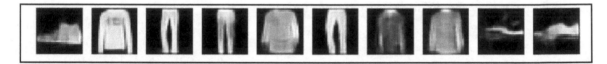

The denoiser has made a reasonable attempt of getting our images back, considering the extent to which they were initially blurred out.

TensorBoard output

To see the TensorBoard output, use the following on your command line:

```
tensorboard  --logdir=./tmp/tb
```

You will then need to point your browser at http://localhost:6006.

The following graphs show the loss (*y*-axis) as a function of epoch (*x*-axis) for training and validation:

The following graph shows the training loss:

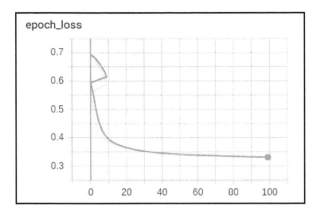

The validation loss is shown in the next graph:

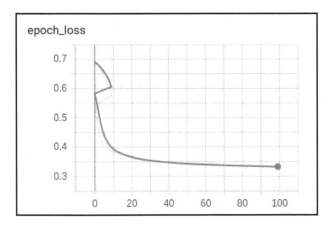

That concludes our look at autoencoders.

Summary

In this chapter, we looked at two applications of autoencoders in unsupervised learning: firstly for compressing data, and secondly for denoising, meaning the removal of noise from images.

In the next chapter, we will look at how neural networks are used in image processing and identification.

3
Section 3: Neural Network Applications of TensorFlow 2.00 Alpha

In this section, we will look at a number of **artificial neural network (ANN)** applications. These include image recognition, neural style transfer, text style generation, fashion recognition, and semantic analysis of the IMDb database of film reviews.

This section contains the following chapters:

- Chapter 6, *Recognizing Images with TensorFlow 2*
- Chapter 7, *Neural Style Transfer Using TensorFlow 2*
- Chapter 8, *Recurrent Neural Networks Using Tensorflow 2*
- Chapter 9, *TensorFlow Estimators and TensorFlow Hub*

6
Recognizing Images with TensorFlow 2

This chapter is in two sections, but we will be learning about image classification using TensorFlow in both.

In this chapter, we will cover the following main topics:

- Quick Draw – image classification using TensorFlow
- CIFAR 10 image classification using TensorFlow

In the first section, we will develop a TensorFlow 2 model for image recognition using the technologies we learned about in the previous chapters—in particular, `Chapter 2`, *Keras, a High-Level API for TensorFlow 2*. This will allow us to see how all of the relevant techniques are brought together to create, train, and evaluate a complete model using TensorFlow 2. We will make use of the Quick Draw! image dataset from Google to help with this.

Quick Draw – image classification using TensorFlow

We will be using images taken from Google's Quick Draw! dataset. This is a public, that is, open source, the dataset of 50 million images in 345 categories, all of which were drawn in 20 seconds or less by over 15 million users taking part in the challenge. We will train on 10,000 images in 10 categories, some of which were chosen to be similar so that we can test the discriminatory power of the model. You can see examples of these images at `https://quickdraw.withgoogle.com/data`. The images are available in a variety of formats, all of which are described at `https://github.com/googlecreativelab/quickdraw-dataset`.

Here, we will use the images that have been stored as `.npy` files. The public dataset of `.npy` files is hosted at `https://console.cloud.google.com/storage/browser/quickdraw_dataset/full/numpy_bitmap?pli=1`. From here, they can be downloaded one set at a time. To run this example with different images, delete the image files from the data directory and download the images you want into the same directory in the repository. The program reads the labels from the filenames.

In this section, we will cover the following topics:

- Acquiring the data
- Preprocessing the data
- Creating the model
- Training and testing the model
- Saving, loading, and retesting the model
- Saving and loading NumPy image data using the .h5 format
- Loading a pre-trained model
- Working with a pre-trained model

We will develop and present the code in short snippets as we go along. These snippets are bolted together into a complete program in the repository (`https://github.com/PacktPublishing/Tensorflow-2-0-Quick-Start-Guide`).

Acquiring the data

We will need to download the data from Google. There is an empty directory called `data_files` that you can download the data into.

Go to `https://console.cloud.google.com/storage/browser/quickdraw_dataset/full/numpy_bitmap?pli=1` and download 10 datasets into the `data_files` folder. The following is an example of the files that will be downloaded:

```
'alarm_clock.npy', 'broom.npy', 'ant.npy', 'bee.npy', 'cell_phone.npy',
'baseball.npy', 'dolphin.npy', 'crocodile.npy', 'aircraft_carrier.npy',
'asparagus.npy'
```

The files you will download will have prepended extra bits on their names, such as `full_numpy_bitmap_alarm clock.npy`.

To make these more concise, remove the bit at the beginning and rename the file so that the filename becomes, in our example, just `alarm_clock.npy`. Do this for all 10 files.

Setting up our environment

First, we need to import the dependencies:

```
import tensorflow as tf
import keras
import numpy as np
from sklearn.model_selection import train_test_split
from os import walk
```

You may need to run `pip install sklearn`. Next, we will establish some constants for later use:

```
batch_size = 128
img_rows, img_cols = 28, 28 # image dimensions
```

Next, we will use the `os.walk` method to collect the filenames of datasets from the `data_files` folder:

 Note that the filenames are collected in the list variable `filenames`.

```
data_path = "data_files/"
for (dirpath, dirnames, filenames) in walk(data_path):
    pass # filenames accumulate in list 'filenames'
print(filenames)
```

The filenames (which correspond to the `label` categories) are as follows for our example:

```
['alarm_clock.npy', 'broom.npy', 'ant.npy', 'bee.npy', 'cell_phone.npy',
'baseball.npy', 'dolphin.npy', 'crocodile.npy', 'aircraft_carrier.npy',
'asparagus.npy']
```

To run this example with different images, simply download 10 different files into the `data` folder.

Next, we will define some more values that are required by the model. The total number of images (`num_images`) may be changed here:

```
num_images = 1000000 ### was 100000, reduce this number if memory issues.
num_files = len(filenames) # *** we have 10 files ***
images_per_category = num_images//num_files
seed = np.random.randint(1, 10e7)
i=0
print(images_per_category)
```

Preprocessing the data

Next comes the code that loads the images into memory. We will loop through the files and, after getting the value of the path to the file, load that file or set of images (x). Then, we cast x into a float and divide by 255 to bring it into the range of 0 to 1. After that, we create a numeric label, y, for that set of images, x. This will be 0 for the first set of images, 1 for the next set, all the way up to 9 for the final set, controlled by the variable i. We then slice the sets x and y to get the images and labels back into x and y. After that, we accumulate x and y into x_all and y_all, creating these two new lists if this is their first time in the loop (that is, i=0) and concatenating x and y onto them if it is not their first time through the loop (that is, i>0). When this loop terminates, x_all and y_all will contain the images with their labels, respectively:

```
i=0
for file in filenames:
    file_path = data_path + file
    x = np.load(file_path)
    x = x.astype('float32') ##normalize images
    x /= 255.0
    y = [i] * len(x) # create numeric label for this image

    x = x[:images_per_category] # get the sample of images
    y = y[:images_per_category] # get the sample of labels

    if i == 0:
        x_all = x
        y_all = y
    else:
        x_all = np.concatenate((x,x_all), axis=0)
        y_all = np.concatenate((y,y_all), axis=0)
    i += 1
```

After this, we will split x_all and y_all into train and test sets by using the train_test_split method from the sklearn.model_selection module with an 80/20 train/test split:

```
#split data arrays into train and test segments
x_train, x_test, y_train, y_test = train_test_split(x_all, y_all,
test_size=0.2, random_state=42)
```

Since we are going to use a convolutional neural network (convNet) to categorize the Quick Draw! images, the next thing to do is reshape x_train and x_test into the 28 x 28 x 1 images they started out life as, where the first two dimensions are the height and width of the image in pixels and the third dimension represents a grayscale at each of the pixels. We will also establish the input_shape, which we will use in the first layer of the convNet:

```
x_train = x_train.reshape(x_train.shape[0], img_rows, img_cols, 1)
x_test = x_test.reshape(x_test.shape[0], img_rows, img_cols, 1)
input_shape = (img_rows, img_cols, 1)
```

After this, we will one-hot encode the y_train and y_test labels, as required by the convNet:

```
y_train = tf.keras.utils.to_categorical(y_train, num_files)
y_test = tf.keras.utils.to_categorical(y_test, num_files)
```

Next, we will further split the training and test x sets into smaller test sets, together with the validation sets, with a 90/10 split:

```
x_train, x_valid, y_train, y_valid = train_test_split(x_train, y_train,
test_size=0.1, random_state=42)
```

Creating the model

Now, we are ready to create the convNet model.

There are two convolutional layers (with a ReLU activation), each of which is interposed with maxpooling and dropout layers, followed by a layer to flatten the output of the convolutional layers into one dimension. These layers are followed by a dense (fully connected) one-dimensional layer (again with a ReLU activation), a final dropout layer, and lastly a softmax layer with 10 units. The activation of each output unit in the softmax layer gives the probability that the image is one of the 10 images. There is plenty of room for experimentation with this ANN architecture.

The model is then compiled using a loss of categorical cross-entropy:

```
model = tf.keras.Sequential()

model.add(tf.keras.layers.Conv2D(32, kernel_size=(3, 3), activation='relu',
input_shape=input_shape))
model.add(tf.keras.layers.MaxPooling2D(pool_size=(2, 2)))
model.add(tf.keras.layers.Dropout(0.25))

model.add(tf.keras.layers.Conv2D(64, (3, 3), activation='relu'))
```

```
model.add(tf.keras.layers.MaxPooling2D(pool_size=(2, 2)))
model.add(tf.keras.layers.Dropout(0.25))

model.add(tf.keras.layers.Flatten())
model.add(tf.keras.layers.Dense(128, activation='relu'))
model.add(tf.keras.layers.Dropout(0.5))
model.add(tf.keras.layers.Dense(num_files, activation='softmax'))

print("Compiling...........")
model.compile(loss=tf.keras.losses.categorical_crossentropy,
  optimizer=tf.keras.optimizers.Adadelta(),
  metrics=['accuracy'])
```

Training and testing the model

We are now in a position to train the model using the `fit` method. Note the use of the validation set, which is distinct from the training set. The `callbacks` list can also be used for operations such as saving the best model or terminating training when learning has stopped if this happens before all the epochs have finished. See `https://keras.io/callbacks/` for details:

```
epochs=25
callbacks=[tf.keras.callbacks.TensorBoard(logdir = "./tb_log_dir")]
model.fit( x_train, y_train,
  batch_size=batch_size,
  epochs=epochs,
  callbacks=callbacks,
  verbose=1,
  validation_data=(x_valid, y_valid)
  )
```

Depending on the hardware configuration the model finds itself in, this model will train quite quickly if it's running on a GPU, or slowly on a CPU. The number of epochs may be reduced for demonstrative purposes. On an NVIDIA GTX 1080 GPU, the time/epoch was about 38 seconds.

To determine the accuracy of the model, the `evaluate` method is used as follows. Note that the test set is used for this evaluation:

```
score = model.evaluate(x_test, y_test, verbose=1)
print('Test loss:', score[0])
print('Test accuracy:', score[1])
```

We can also take a random sample of test images and see how the model fared with the following code. The labels are retrieved from the filenames and printed for reference before pairs of predicted versus actual labels are printed:

```
import os
labels = [os.path.splitext(file)[0] for file in filenames]
print(labels)
print("\nFor each pair in the following, the first label is predicted,
second is actual\n")
for i in range(20):
    t = np.random.randint(len(x_test) )
    x1= x_test[t]
    x1 = x1.reshape(1,28,28,1)
    p = model.predict(x1)
    print("-------------------------")
    print(labels[np.argmax(p)])
    print(labels[np.argmax(y_test[t])])
    print("-------------------------")
```

TensorBoard callback

TensorBoard is a visualization tool for trained models. The full signature of the TensorBoard callback is as follows:

```
tf.keras.callbacks.TensorBoard(log_dir='./logs', histogram_freq=0,
batch_size=32, write_graph=True, write_grads=False, write_images=False,
embeddings_freq=0, embeddings_layer_names=None, embeddings_metadata=None,
embeddings_data=None, update_freq='epoch')
```

There is a very clear and detailed description of all of these arguments at https://keras. io/callbacks/. TensorBoard may be invoked from the command line like so:

tensorboard --logdir=/full_path_to_your_logs

For example, we can use `tensorboard --logdir=./logs` for the default directory. Setting `histogram_freq` to anything other than 0 causes a significant pause between `epochs` while the data is written, and should only be used if the activation and weight histograms for all of the layers of the model are required.

Saving, loading, and retesting the model

Now, we can save the model and delete it:

```
model.save("./QDrawModel.h5")
del model
```

Then, we need to reload it:

```
from tensorflow.keras.models import load_model
model = load_model('./QDrawModel.h5')
```

Finally, we have to summarize it to show that we have successfully reloaded the saved model:

```
model.summary()
```

Lastly, we print out a test sample of 20 items of fashion to ensure that the network is working as it should:

```
print("For each pair, first is predicted, second is actual")
for i in range(20):
    t = np.random.randint(len(x_test))
    x1= x_test[t]
    x1 = x1.reshape(1,28,28,1)
    p = model.predict(x1)
    print("------------------------")
    print(labels[np.argmax(p)])
    print(labels[np.argmax(y_test[t])])
    print("------------------------")
```

Saving and loading NumPy image data using the .h5 format

Should there be a requirement to save the training and test data from the previous program, the following code can be used:

```
import h5py
with h5py.File('x_train.h5', 'w') as hf:
    hf.create_dataset("QuickDraw", data=x_train)
with h5py.File('y_train.h5', 'w') as hf:
    hf.create_dataset("QuickDraw", data=y_train)
with h5py.File('x_test.h5', 'w') as hf:
    hf.create_dataset("QuickDraw", data=x_test)
with h5py.File('y_test.h5', 'w') as hf:
```

```
    hf.create_dataset("QuickDraw", data-y_test)
```

Note that the dataset name that's passed to the `h5py.File()` method when loading a dataset must be the same as what was used when the dataset was saved with the `h5py.File.create_dataset()` method:

```
import h5py
hf = h5py.File('x_train.h5', 'r')
x_train = np.array(hf["QuickDraw"][:])
hf = h5py.File('x_test.h5', 'r')
x_test = np.array(hf["QuickDraw"][:])
hf = h5py.File('y_train.h5', 'r')
y_train = np.array(hf["QuickDraw"][:])
hf = h5py.File('y_test.h5', 'r')
y_test = np.array(hf["QuickDraw"][:])
```

Loading and inference with a pre-trained model

The trained model, `'QDrawModel.h5'`, which has been run for 25 epochs and achieved a test accuracy of just over 90%, has been saved in the repository. You have already seen this code; it is reproduced here for your convenience.

So, to reiterate, you can load this trained model with the following code:

```
from keras.models import load_model
model = load_model('./QDrawModel.h5')
model.summary()
```

Again, the training/test data can be loaded with the following code:

```
import h5py
import numpy as np
hf = h5py.File('x_train.h5', 'r')
x_train = np.array(hf["QuickDraw"][:])
hf = h5py.File('x_test.h5', 'r')
x_test = np.array(hf["QuickDraw"][:])
hf = h5py.File('y_train.h5', 'r')
y_train = np.array(hf["QuickDraw"][:])
hf = h5py.File('y_test.h5', 'r')
y_test = np.array(hf["QuickDraw"][:])
```

Reiterating again, we can get the labels (which we have seen correspond to the image filenames) with the following code:

```python
from os import walk
import os
data_path = "data_files/" # folder for image files
for (dirpath, dirnames, filenames) in walk(data_path):
  pass # filenames accumulate in list 'filenames'
labels = [os.path.splitext(file)[0] for file in filenames]
print(labels)
```

Inference using our loaded model may then be achieved with the following code. Note that this also demonstrates how to force computation to take place on a CPU, should that be a requirement:

```python
import tensorflow as tf
with tf.device('/cpu:0'):
    for i in range(10):
        t = np.random.randint(len(x_test) )
        x1= x_test[t]
        x1 = x1.reshape(1,28,28,1)
        p = model.predict(x1)
        y1 = y_test[t]
        print("------------------------")
        print(labels[np.argmax([p])])
        print(labels[y1])
        print("------------------------")
```

CIFAR 10 image classification using TensorFlow

In this second section, we will look at training a model to recognize images in the CIFAR10 image dataset. This will give us the chance to exemplify a slightly different style of sequential model creation.

Introduction

The CIFAR 10 image dataset, with 10 categories, is a labeled subset of the 80 million tiny images dataset. These images were collected by Alex Krizhevsky, Vinod Nair, and Geoffrey Hinton. Full details on this dataset can be found at https://www.cs.toronto.edu/~kriz/cifar.html.

In total, there are 60,000 32 x 32 color images in the 10 classes consisting of 50,000 training images and 10,000 test images.

The categories are as follows:

```
labels =
['airplane','automobile','bird','cat','deer','dog','frog','horse','ship','t
ruck']
```

Here are a few examples of images from these categories:

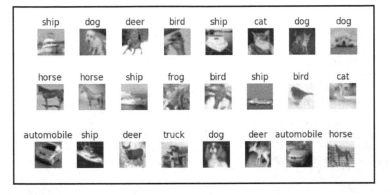

The application

First, here are the imports to set things up:

```
import tensorflow as tf
import numpy as np
from tensorflow.keras.datasets import cifar10
from tensorflow.keras.preprocessing.image import ImageDataGenerator
from tensorflow.keras.models import Sequential
from tensorflow.keras.layers import Dense, Dropout, Activation, Flatten
from tensorflow.keras.layers import Conv2D, MaxPooling2D,BatchNormalization
from tensorflow.keras import regularizers
from tensorflow.keras.models import load_model
import os
from matplotlib import pyplot as plt
from PIL import Image
```

You may need to run `pip install PIL`.

Next, we have a set of values that we will use throughout the rest of the code:

```
batch_size = 32
number_of_classes = 10
epochs = 100 # for testing; use epochs = 100 for training ~30 secs/epoch on
CPU
weight_decay = 1e-4
save_dir = os.path.join(os.getcwd(), 'saved_models')
model_name = 'keras_cifar10_trained_model.h5'
number_of_images = 5
```

Then, we can load and have a look at the shape of the data:

```
(x_train, y_train), (x_test, y_test) = cifar10.load_data()
print('x_train shape:', x_train.shape)
print(x_train.shape[0], 'train samples')
print(x_test.shape[0], 'test samples')
```

This produces the expected output:

x_train shape: (50000, 32, 32, 3) 50000 train samples 10000 test samples

Now, we have a function to display a subset of our images. This will display them in a grid:

```
def show_images(images):
    plt.figure(1)
    image_index = 0
    for i in range(0,number_of_images):
        for j in range(0,number_of_images):
            plt.subplot2grid((number_of_images, number_of_images),(i,j))
            plt.imshow(Image.fromarray(images[image_index]))
            image_index +=1
            plt.gca().axes.get_yaxis().set_visible(False)
            plt.gca().axes.get_xaxis().set_visible(False)
    plt.show()
```

Let's perform a call to the following function:

```
show_images(x_test[:number_of_images*number_of_images])
```

This gives us the following output:

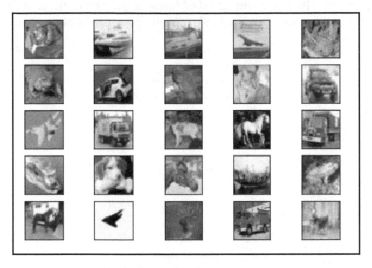

 Note that the images are intentionally small in the original dataset.

Now, we can cast our images on floats and change their range to [0, 1]:

```
x_train = x_train.astype('float32')/255
x_test = x_test.astype('float32')/255
```

Our labels are best learned if they are provided as one-hot vectors, so we will do this now:

```
y_train = tf.keras.utils.to_categorical(y_train, number_of_classes) # or
use tf.one_hot()
y_test = tf.keras.utils.to_categorical(y_test, number_of_classes)
```

Next, we can specify our model's architecture. Note that we have used a slightly different method of specifying activations compared to what we did previously:

```
model.add(Activation('elu'))
```

The elu activation function stands for Exponential Linear Unit. It is well described at https://sefiks.com/2018/01/02/elu-as-a-neural-networks-activation-function/.

Notice that we are using a Sequential model with Convolutional, `BatchNormalization`, and MaxPooling layers. The penultimate layer flattens the structure and the final layer uses a softmax activation so that our predicted class will show up as the output neuron with the highest activation:

```
model = Sequential()
model.add(Conv2D(32, (3,3), padding='same',
kernel_regularizer=regularizers.l2(weight_decay),
input_shape=x_train.shape[1:]))
model.add(Activation('elu'))
model.add(BatchNormalization())
model.add(Conv2D(32, (3,3), padding='same',
kernel_regularizer=regularizers.l2(weight_decay)))
model.add(Activation('elu'))
model.add(BatchNormalization())
model.add(MaxPooling2D(pool_size=(2,2)))
model.add(Dropout(0.2))

model.add(Conv2D(64, (3,3), padding='same',
kernel_regularizer=regularizers.l2(weight_decay)))
model.add(Activation('elu'))
model.add(BatchNormalization())
model.add(Conv2D(64, (3,3), padding='same',
kernel_regularizer=regularizers.l2(weight_decay)))
model.add(Activation('elu'))
model.add(BatchNormalization())
model.add(MaxPooling2D(pool_size=(2,2)))
model.add(Dropout(0.3))

model.add(Conv2D(128, (3,3), padding='same',
kernel_regularizer=regularizers.l2(weight_decay)))
model.add(Activation('elu'))
model.add(BatchNormalization())
model.add(Conv2D(128, (3,3), padding='same',
kernel_regularizer=regularizers.l2(weight_decay)))
model.add(Activation('elu'))
model.add(BatchNormalization())
model.add(MaxPooling2D(pool_size=(2,2)))
model.add(Dropout(0.4))

model.add(Flatten())
model.add(Dense(number_of_classes, activation='softmax'))
```

Next, we must define our optimizer; `RMSprop`. `decay` is the rate at which the learning rate is reduced over each update:

```
opt = tf.keras.optimizers.RMSprop(lr=0.0001, decay=decay)
```

Now, we will compile our model:

```
model.compile(loss='categorical_crossentropy',
optimizer=opt,metrics=['accuracy'])
```

To help the model learn and generalize, we are going to implement real-time data augmentation.

This is done with the `ImageDataGenerator()` function. Its signature is as follows:

```
keras.preprocessing.image.ImageDataGenerator(featurewise_center=False,
samplewise_center=False, featurewise_std_normalization=False,
samplewise_std_normalization=False, zca_whitening=False, zca_epsilon=1e-06,
rotation_range=0, width_shift_range=0.0, height_shift_range=0.0,
brightness_range=None, shear_range=0.0, zoom_range=0.0,
channel_shift_range=0.0, fill_mode='nearest', cval=0.0,
horizontal_flip=False, vertical_flip=False, rescale=None,
preprocessing_function=None, data_format=None, validation_split=0.0,
dtype=None)
```

However, we will mainly use the defaults as seen in the preceding signature. The data will be looped over in batches.

What this does is apply various transformations to the images, such as horizontal flips, height shifts, width shifts, rotations, and so on. We will use the following code to demonstrate this:

```
# This will do preprocessing and real-time data augmentation:
datagen = ImageDataGenerator(
 rotation_range=10, # randomly rotate images in the range 0 to 10 degrees

 width_shift_range=0.1,# randomly shift images horizontally (fraction of
total width)

 height_shift_range=0.1,# randomly shift images vertically (fraction of
total height)

 horizontal_flip=True, # randomly flip images

 validation_split=0.1)
```

We will also set up a callback so that if the accuracy of our model stops improving, the training will halt and the best weights will be restored to the model.

The signature of the `EarlyStopping` callback is as follows:

```
keras.callbacks.EarlyStopping(monitor='val_loss', min_delta=0, patience=0,
verbose=0, mode='auto', baseline=None, restore_best_weights=False)
```

`Monitor` is the quantity to be tracked, `min_delta` is the minimum change in the tracked quantity that counts as an improvement, `patience` is the number of epochs with no change after which the training will be halted, and `mode` is one of ['min', 'max', 'auto'], which determines if the tracked value should be decreasing or increasing, or whether that should be determined from its name, respectively. `baseline` is the value for the tracked value to reach, while `restore_best_weights` determines whether the model weights from the best epoch should be restored (if `false`, the most recent weights are used).

We will have the following code:

```
callback = tf.keras.callbacks.EarlyStopping(monitor='accuracy',
min_delta=0, patience=1, verbose=1,mode='max', restore_best_weights=True)
```

Now, we can train our model. The `fit.generator()` function is used to train the model on data that's presented in batches by the `flow()` generator. More details can be found at https://keras.io/models/sequential/#fit_generator:

```
model.fit_generator(datagen.flow(x_train, y_train, batch_size=batch_size),
epochs=epochs, callbacks=[callback])
```

Let's save our model so that it can be reloaded at a later date:

```
if not os.path.isdir(save_dir):
  os.makedirs(save_dir)

model_path = os.path.join(save_dir, model_name)
model.save(model_path)
print('Model saved at: %s ' % model_path)
```

Let's now reload it:

```
model1 = tf.keras.models.load_model(model_path)
model1.summary()
```

Finally, let's see how our model fares on our test set. We need to reload the data, because it has been mangled:

```
(x_train, y_train), (x_test, y_test) = cifar10.load_data()
show_images(x_test[:num_images*num_images])
x_test = x_test.astype('float32')/255
```

Here are the labels again:

```
labels =
['airplane','automobile','bird','cat','deer','dog','frog','horse','ship','t
ruck']
```

Finally, we can check the predicted labels:

```
indices =
tf.argmax(input=model1.predict(x_test[:number_of_images*number_of_images]),
axis=1)
i = 0
print('Learned \t True')
print('=====================')
for index in indices:
    print(labels[index], '\t', labels[y_test[i][0]])
    i+=1
```

In a run, the early stopping kicked in at 43 epochs, giving a testing accuracy of 81.4% and the following result for the first 25 images:

```
Learned   True
=====================
cat       cat
ship      ship
ship      ship
ship      airplane
frog      frog
frog      frog
automobile          automobile
frog      frog
cat       cat
automobile          automobile
airplane            airplane
truck     truck
dog       dog
horse     horse
truck     truck
ship      ship
dog       dog
horse     horse
```

```
ship       ship
frog       frog
horse      horse
airplane              airplane
deer       deer
truck      truck
deer       dog
```

This accuracy could be improved with further tweaks to the model architecture and hyperparameters, such as the learning rate.

That concludes our look at the CIFAR 10 image dataset.

Summary

This chapter was divided into two sections. In the first section, we investigated the Quick Draw! dataset from Google. We introduced it and then we saw how to load it into memory. This was straightforward as Google has kindly made the dataset available as a set of .npy files, which can be loaded directly into NumPy arrays. Next, we divided the data into training, validation, and test sets. After creating our ConvNet model, we trained it on the data and tested it. In the tests, over 25 epochs, the model achieved an accuracy of just over 90%, and we noted that this could probably be improved upon with further tweaking of the model. Lastly, we saw how to save a trained model and then how to reload it and use it for further inference.

In the second section, we trained a model to recognize images in the CIFAR 10 image dataset. This dataset consists of 10 classes of images and is a popular one for testing architectures and for hyperparameter investigations. We achieved an accuracy of just over 81%.

In the next chapter, we will investigate neural style transfer, which involves taking the content of one image and imposing the style of a second image onto it to produce a third, hybrid image.

7
Neural Style Transfer Using TensorFlow 2

Neural style transfer is a technique whereby the artistic style of one image is imposed on the content of another image using a neural network, so that what you end up with is a hybrid of the two images. The image you start with is called the **content image**. The image whose style you impose on the content image is known as the **style reference image**. Google refers to the transformed image as the **input image**, which seems confusing (input in the sense that it takes input from two different sources); let's instead refer to it as the **hybrid image**. So, the hybrid image is the content image with the style of the style reference image imposed on it.

Neural style transfer works by defining two loss functions—one that describes the difference between the content of two images and another that describes the difference in style between two images.

To begin the procedure, the hybrid image is initialized with the content image. Then, the differences (also known as losses or distances) between the content and style of the content and hybrid image are minimized using backpropagation. This creates a new image (that is, a hybrid image) with the style of the style reference image, and the content of the content image.

There are a few techniques involved here in this procedure—use of the Functional API, the use of a pre-trained model and its feature maps, and the use of a custom training loop for minimizing the `loss` functions. We will meet all of these in the code that follows.

There are a couple of prerequisites to getting the most out of this technique—the original paper by Gatys et al, 2015, `https://arxiv.org/abs/1508.06576`, whilst not essential, does explain the technique very well, and an understanding of reducing loss by gradient descent is pretty much necessary.

We will be using feature layers from the VGG19 architecture (which was trained on the famed ImageNet dataset, with over 14 million images and 1,000 categories).

The code we will examine is derived from that provided by Google; it uses eager execution, which of course we do not need to code for, since it is the default in TensorFlow 2. This code runs much faster on a GPU, but is still trainable in reasonable time on a CPU, given a little patience.

In this chapter, we will cover the following topics:

- Setting up the imports
- Preprocessing the images
- Viewing the original images
- Using the VGG19 architecture
- Creating the model
- Calculating the losses
- Performing the style transfer

Setting up the imports

To use this implementation with your own images, you need to save those images in the `./tmp/nst` directory in your downloaded repository, then edit the `content_path` and `style_path` paths, shown in the following code.

As usual, the first thing we need to do is to import (and configure) the required modules:

```
import numpy as np
from PIL import Image
import time
import functools

import matplotlib.pyplot as plt
import matplotlib as mpl
# set things up for images display
mpl.rcParams['figure.figsize'] = (10,10)
mpl.rcParams['axes.grid'] = False
```

You may need to `pip install pillow`, which is a fork of PIL. Next comes the TensorFlow modules:

```
import tensorflow as tf

from tensorflow.keras.preprocessing import image as kp_image
from tensorflow.keras import models
from tensorflow.keras import losses
from tensorflow.keras import layers
```

```
from tensorflow.keras import backend as K
from tensorflow.keras import optimizers
```

Here are the two images we will initially work with:

```
content_path = './tmp/nst/elephant.jpg'#Andrew Shiva / Wikipedia / CC BY-SA
4.0
style_path = './tmp/nst/zebra.jpg' # zebra:Yathin S Krishnappa,
https://creativecommons.org/licenses/by-sa/4.0/deed.en
```

Preprocessing the images

The next function loads an image, with a little preprocessing. Image.open() is what's known as a lazy operation. The function finds the file and opens it for reading, but the image data isn't actually read from the file until you try to process it or load the data. The next group of three lines resizes the image, so that the maximum dimension in either direction is 512 (max_dimension) pixels. For example, if the image were 1,024 x 768, scale would be 0.5 (512/1,024), and this would be applied to both dimensions of the image, giving a resized image size of 512 x 384. The Image.ANTIALIAS argument preserves the best quality of the image. Next, the PIL image is converted into a NumPy array using the img_to_array() call (a method of tensorflow.keras.preprocessing).

Finally, to be compatible with later usage, the image needs a batch dimension along axis zero, (giving four dimensions altogether since the image is in color). This is achieved with the call to np.expand_dims():

```
def load_image(path_to_image):
    max_dimension = 512
    image = Image.open(path_to_image)
    longest_side = max(image.size)
    scale = max_dimension/longest_side
    image = image.resize((round(image.size[0]*scale),
round(image.size[1]*scale)), Image.ANTIALIAS)
    image = kp_image.img_to_array(image) # keras preprocessing
    # Broadcast the image array so that it has a batch dimension on axis 0
    image = np.expand_dims(image, axis=0)
    return image
```

The next function displays an image that has been preprocessed by `load_image()`. Since we don't need the extra dimension for display purposes, it is removed with a call to `np.squeeze()`. After that, the values in the image data are converted into unsigned 8-bit integer as required by the call to `plt.imshow()` that follows with an optional title:

```
def show_image(image, title=None):
    # Remove the batch dimension from the image
    image1 = np.squeeze(image, axis=0)
    # Normalize the image for display
    image1 = image1.astype('uint8')
    plt.imshow(image1)
    if title is not None:
        plt.title(title)
    plt.imshow(image1)
```

Viewing the original images

Next, we use calls to the two preceding functions to display our content and style images, remembering that the image pixels need to be of type unsigned 8-bit integer. The `plt.subplot(1,2,1)` function means use a grid of one row and two columns at position one; `plt.subplot(1,2,2)` means use a grid of one row and two columns at position two:

```
channel_means = [103.939, 116.779, 123.68] # means of the BGR channels, for
VGG processing

plt.figure(figsize=(10,10))

content_image = load_image(content_path).astype('uint8')
style_image = load_image(style_path).astype('uint8')

plt.subplot(1, 2, 1)
show_image(content_image, 'Content Image')

plt.subplot(1, 2, 2)
show_image(style_image, 'Style Image')

plt.show()
```

The output is shown in the following screenshot:

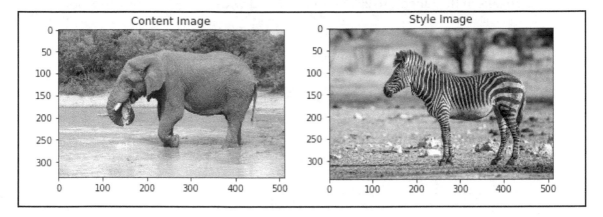

There follows a function to load the image. As we are going to use this, as mentioned, with the vgg19 trained model, we need to preprocess our image data accordingly.

The tf.keras module provides us with a method to do this. The preprocessing here flips our RGB color image to BGR:

```
def load_and_process_image(path_to_image):
    image = load_image(path_to_image)
    image = tf.keras.applications.vgg19.preprocess_input(image)
    return image
```

For displaying our image, we need to have a function that takes data processed with load_and_process_image and returns the image data to its original state. This has to be done manually.

Firstly, we check that the image has the correct number of dimensions, and raise an error if this is not three or four.

The preprocessing subtracts from each channel its mean, so then the mean of the channel is zero. The value subtracted comes from the ImageNet analysis, where the means of the BGR channels are 103.939, 116.779, and 123.68, respectively.

So next, we add these values back to the BGR (color) channel to restore the original values, and then flip the BGR sequence back to RGB.

Finally, for this function, we need to make sure that our values are unsigned, 8-bit integers whose value falls in the range 0 to 255; this is achieved with the `np.clip()` function:

```
def deprocess_image(processed_image):
  im = processed_image.copy()
  if len(im.shape) == 4:
    im = np.squeeze(im, 0)
  assert len(im.shape) == 3, ("Input to deprocess image must be an image of
"
                              "dimension [1, height, width, channel] or
[height, width, channel]")
  if len(im.shape) != 3:
    raise ValueError("Invalid input to deprocessing image")

  # the inverse of the preprocessing step
  im[:, :, 0] += channel_means[0] # these are the means subtracted by the
preprocessing step
  im[:, :, 1] += channel_means[1]
  im[:, :, 2] += channel_means[2]
  im= im[:, :, ::-1] # channel last

  im = np.clip(im, 0, 255).astype('uint8')
  return im
```

Using the VGG19 architecture

The best way to understand the next snippet is to have a look at the VGG19 architecture. Here is a good place: `https://github.com/fchollet/deep-learning-models/blob/master/vgg19.py` (about half way down the page).

Here, you will see that VGG19 is a fairly straightforward architecture, consisting of blocks of convolutional layers with a max pooling layer at the end of each block.

For the content layer, we use the second convolutional layer in `block5`. This highest block is used because the earlier blocks have feature maps more representative of individual pixels; higher layers in the network capture the high-level content in terms of objects and their arrangement in the input image, but do not constrain the actual exact pixel values of the reconstruction (see Gatys et al, 2015, `https://arxiv.org/abs/1508.06576`, cited previously).

For the style layers, we are going to use the first convolutional layer in each block of layers, that is, `block1_conv1` up to `block5_conv5`.

The length of the content and of the style layers are then saved for later use:

```
# The feature maps are obtained from this content layer
content_layers = ['block5_conv2']

# Style layers we need
style_layers = ['block1_conv1',
                'block2_conv1',
                'block3_conv1',
                'block4_conv1',
                'block5_conv1'
                ]

number_of_content_layers = len(content_layers)
number_of_style_layers = len(style_layers)
```

Creating the model

There now follows a series of functions leading eventually up to the main function that performs the style transfer (`run_style_transfer()`).

The first function in this sequence, `get_model()`, creates the model we are going to use.

It first loads trained `vgg_model` (which has been trained on `ImageNet`) without its classification layer (`include_top=False`). Next, it freezes the loaded model (`vgg_model.trainable = False`).

The style and content layer output values are then acquired using list comprehensions, which iterate over the names of the layers that we specified in the previous section.

These output values are then used, together with the VGG input to create our new model with access to VGG layers, that is, `get_model()` returns a Keras model that outputs the style and content intermediate layers of the trained VGG19 model. It is unnecessary to use the top layer, as this is the final classification layer in VGG19, which we will not be using.

We are going to create an output image so that the distance (difference) between the output and the input/style on corresponding feature layers is minimized:

```
def get_model():
 vgg_model = tf.keras.applications.vgg19.VGG19(include_top=False,
weights='imagenet')
 vgg_model.trainable = False

 # Acquire the output layers corresponding to the style layers and the
content layers
 style_outputs = [vgg_model.get_layer(name).output for name in
style_layers]
 content_outputs = [vgg_model.get_layer(name).output for name in
content_layers]
 model_outputs = style_outputs + content_outputs

# Build model
 return models.Model(vgg_model.input, model_outputs)
```

Calculating the losses

We now need the losses between the contents and styles of the two images. We will be using the mean squared loss as follows. Notice here that the subtraction in `image1 - image2` is element-wise between the two image arrays. This subtraction works because the images have been resized to the same size in `load_image`:

```
def rms_loss(image1,image2):
    loss = tf.reduce_mean(input_tensor=tf.square(image1 - image2))
    return loss
```

So next, we define our `content_loss` function. This is just the mean squared difference between what is named `content` and `target` in the function signature:

```
def content_loss(content, target):
   return rms_loss(content, target)
```

The style loss is defined in terms of a quantity called a **Gram matrix**. A Gram matrix, also known as the metric, is the dot product of the style matrix with its own transpose. Since this means that each column of the image matrix is multiplied with each row, we can think of the spatial information that was contained in the original representations to have been *distributed*. The result is non-localized information about the image, such as texture, shapes, and weights, that is, its style.

The code to produce `gram_matrix` is as follows:

```
def gram_matrix(input_tensor):
  channels = int(input_tensor.shape[-1]) # channels is last dimension
  tensor = tf.reshape(input_tensor, [-1, channels]) # Make the image
channels first
  number_of_channels = tf.shape(input=tensor)[0] # number of channels
  gram = tf.matmul(tensor, tensor, transpose_a=True) # produce
tensor^T*tensor
  return gram / tf.cast(number_of_channels, tf.float32) # scaled by the
number of channels.
```

So then, the style loss (where `gram_target` will be the Gram matrix of the style activations on the hybrid image) is simply as follows:

```
def style_loss(style, gram_target):
  gram_style = gram_matrix(style)
  return rms_loss(gram_style, gram_target)
```

Next, we find the `content_features` and `style_features` representations by getting `content_image` and `style_image` and feeding them through the model. This code is in two blocks, one for `content_features`, and one for `style_features`. For the contents block, we load an image, call our model on it, and lastly, extract the feature layers that were previously assigned. The code for `style_features` is identical, except that we first load the style image:

```
def get_feature_representations(model, content_path, style_path):
  #Function to compute content and style feature representations.

  content_image = load_and_process_image(content_path)
  content_outputs = model(content_image)
  #content_features = [content_layer[0] for content_layer in
content_outputs[:number_of_content_layers]]
  content_features = [content_layer[0] for content_layer in
content_outputs[number_of_style_layers:]]


  style_image = load_and_process_image(style_path)
  style_outputs = model(style_image)
  style_features = [style_layer[0] for style_layer in
style_outputs[:number_of_style_layers]]

  return style_features, content_features
```

Next, we need to compute the total loss. Looking at the signature of the method, we can see that, first, we pass in our model (that gives access to the intermediate layers of VGG19). Next, come `loss_weights`, which are the weights of each contribution of each of the loss functions (`content_weight`, `style_weight`, and total variational weight). Then, we have the initial image, that is, the image we are updating with the optimization process. This is followed by `gram_style_features` and the `content_features`, corresponding to the style layers and content layers, respectively, that we are using.

Firstly copy the style and `content_weight` from the method signature. Then, call the model on our initial image. Our model is directly callable because we are using eager execution, which as we have seen is the default in TensorFlow 2. This call returns all of the model output values.

Then we have two similar blocks, one for content and one for the style. For the first (content) block, get the content and style representations in our desired layers. Next, we accumulate the content losses from all content loss layers, where the contribution of each layer is equally weighted.

The second block is similar to the first block, except that here we accumulate the style losses from all style loss layers, where each contribution of each loss layer is equally weighted.

Finally, the function returns the total loss, the style loss, and the content loss, as shown in the following code:

```
def compute_total_loss(model, loss_weights, init_image,
gram_style_features, content_features):

    style_weight, content_weight = loss_weights
    model_outputs = model(init_image)

    content_score = 0
    content_output_features = model_outputs[number_of_style_layers:]
    weight_per_content_layer = 1.0 / float(number_of_content_layers)
    for target_content, comb_content in zip(content_features,
content_output_features):
        content_score +=
weight_per_content_layer*content_loss(comb_content[0], target_content)
    content_score *= content_weight

    style_score = 0
    style_output_features = model_outputs[:number_of_style_layers]
    weight_per_style_layer = 1.0 / float(number_of_style_layers)
    for target_style, comb_style in zip(gram_style_features,
style_output_features):
        style_score += weight_per_style_layer *style_loss(comb_style[0],
```

```
    target_style)
      style_score *= style_weight

  total_loss = style_score + content_score
  return total_loss, style_score, content_score
```

Next, we have a function that computes the gradients:

```
def compute_grads(config):
  with tf.GradientTape() as tape:
    all_loss = compute_total_loss(**config)
  # Compute gradients wrt input image
  total_loss = all_loss[0]
  return tape.gradient(total_loss, config['init_image']), all_loss

import IPython.display
```

Performing the style transfer

The function that performs `style_transfer` is quite long so we will present it in sections. Its signature is as follows:

```
def run_style_transfer(content_path,
                       style_path,
                       number_of_iterations=1000,
                       content_weight=1e3,
                       style_weight=1e-2):
```

Since we don't want to actually train any layers in our model, just use the output values from the layers as described previously; we set their trainable properties accordingly:

```
model = get_model()
for layer in model.layers:
  layer.trainable = False
```

Next, we get the `style_features` and `content_features` representations from the layers of our model, using the function previously defined:

```
style_features, content_features = get_feature_representations(model,
content_path, style_path)
```

And `gram_style_features`, using a loop over `style_features`, shown as follows:

```
gram_style_features = [gram_matrix(style_feature) for style_feature in
style_features]
```

Next, we initialize the image that will become the output of the algorithm, that is, the hybrid image (also known as the **pastiche image**), by loading the content image and converting it into a tensor:

```
initial_image = load_and_process_image(content_path)
initial_image = tf.Variable(initial_image, dtype=tf.float32)
```

The next line defines the required `AdamOptimizer` function:

```
optimizer = tf.compat.v1.train.AdamOptimizer(learning_rate=5, beta1=0.99,
epsilon=1e-1)
```

We are going to save `best_image` and `best_loss` as we go along, so initialize variables to store these:

```
 best_loss, best_image = float('inf'), None
```

Next, we set up the dictionary of configuration values that will be passed into the `compute_grads()` function:

```
loss_weights = (style_weight, content_weight)
  config = {
      'model': model,
      'loss_weights': loss_weights,
      'init_image': initial_image,
      'gram_style_features': gram_style_features,
      'content_features': content_features
  }
```

Here are the display constants:

```
number_rows = 2
number_cols = 5
display_interval = number_of_iterations/(number_rows*number_cols)
```

Next, we calculate the image bounds, shown as follows:

```
norm_means = np.array(channel_means)
minimum_vals = -norm_means
maximum_vals = 255 - norm_means
```

This list will store the hybrid images:

```
images = []
```

Next, we start the main image processing loop, as follows:

```
for i in range(number_of_iterations):
```

So next we compute the gradients, calculate the losses, call the optimizer to apply the gradients, and clip the image to our previously calculated bounds:

```
grads, all_loss = compute_grads(config)
loss, style_score, content_score = all_loss
optimizer.apply_gradients([(grads, initial_image)])
clipped_image = tf.clip_by_value(initial_image, minimum_vals,
maximum_vals)
initial_image.assign(clipped_image)
```

We are going to save `best_loss` and `best_image` as we go along, so do this next:

```
if loss < best_loss:
# Update best loss and best image from total loss.
  best_loss = loss
  best_image = deprocess_image(initial_image.numpy()
```

Then, we conditionally save the hybrid image (for a total of 10 images), displaying it together with the training metrics:

```
if i % display_interval== 0:
  # Use the .numpy() method to get the numpy image array, needs eager
execution
  plot_image = initial_image.numpy()
  plot_image = deprocess_image(plot_image)
  images.append(plot_image)
  IPython.display.clear_output(wait=True)
  IPython.display.display_png(Image.fromarray(plot_image))
  print('Iteration: {}'.format(i))
  print('Total loss: {:.4e}, '
        'style loss: {:.4e}, '
        'content loss: {:.4e} '
        .format(loss, style_score, content_score))
```

Finally, for this function, we display all of `best_image` and `best_loss`:

```
IPython.display.clear_output(wait=True)
plt.figure(figsize=(14,4))
for i,image in enumerate(images):
  plt.subplot(number_rows,number_cols,i+1)
  plt.imshow(image)
  plt.xticks([])
  plt.yticks([])

return best_image, best_loss
```

Next, we call the preceding function to get `best_image` and `best_loss` (which also displays the 10 images):

The code for this is as follows:

```
best_image, best_loss = run_style_transfer(content_path, style_path,
number_of_iterations=100)
Image.fromarray(best_image)
```

The following is the display for `best_image`:

Final displays

Finally, we have a function that displays the content and style images together with `best_image`:

```
def show_results(best_image, content_path, style_path,
show_large_final=True):
 plt.figure(figsize=(10, 5))
  content = load_image(content_path)
  style = load_image(style_path)

  plt.subplot(1, 2, 1)
  show_image(content, 'Content Image')

  plt.subplot(1, 2, 2)
  show_image(style, 'Style Image')

  if show_large_final:
    plt.figure(figsize=(10, 10))

    plt.imshow(best_image)
    plt.title('Output Image')
    plt.show()
```

This is followed by a call to that function, as follows:

```
show_results(best_image, content_path, style_path)
```

Summary

That concludes our look at neural style transfer. We saw how to take a content image and a style image and produce a hybrid image. We used layers from the trained VGG19 model to accomplish this.

In the next chapter, we will examine recurrent neural networks; these are networks that can process sequential input values, and where both or either of the input values and output values are of variable length.

8
Recurrent Neural Networks Using TensorFlow 2

One of the main drawbacks with a number of neural network architectures, including ConvNets (CNNs), is that they do not allow for sequential data to be processed. In other words, a complete feature, for example, an image, has to be presented all at once. So the input is a fixed length tensor, and the output has to be a fixed length tensor. Neither do the output values of previous features affect the current feature in any way. Also, all of the input values (and output values) are taken to be independent of one another. For example, in our fashion_mnist model (Chapter 4, *Supervised Machine Learning Using TensorFlow 2*), each input fashion image is independent of, and totally ignorant of, previous images.

Recurrent Neural Networks (**RNNs**) overcome this problem and make a wide range of new applications possible.

In this chapter, we will take a look at the following topics:

- Neural network processing modes
- Recurrent architectures
- An application of RNNs
- The code for our RNN example
- Building and instantiating our model
- Training and using our model

Neural network processing modes

The following diagram illustrates the variety of neural network processing modes:

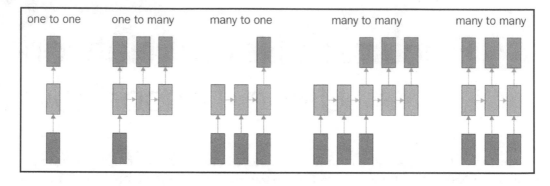

Rectangles represent tensors, arrows represent functions, red is input, blue is output, and green is the tensor state.

From left to right, we have the following:

- Plain feed-forward network, fixed-size input, and fixed-size output, for example, image classification
- Sequence output, for example, image captioning that takes one image and outputs a set of words identifying items in the image
- Sequence input, for example, sentiment identification (like our IMDb application) where a sentence is classed as being of positive or negative sentiment
- Both sequence input and output, for example, machine translation where an RNN takes an English sentence and translates it into a French output
- Synced sequence both input and output, for example, video classification that is like the two, on a frame by frame basis

Recurrent architectures

Hence, a new architecture is required for handling data that arrives sequentially, and where both or either of its input values and output values are of variable length for example, the words in a sentence in a language translation application. In this case, both the input and output to the model are of varying lengths as in the fourth mode previously. Also, in order to predict subsequent words given the current word, previous words need to be known as well. This new neural network architecture is called an RNN, and it is specifically designed to handle sequential data.

The term **recurrent** arises because such models perform the same computation on every element of a sequence, where each output is dependent on previous output. Theoretically, each output depends on all of the previous output items, but in practical terms, RNNs are limited to looking back just a small number of steps. This arrangement is equivalent to an RNN having a memory that can make use of the results of previous calculations.

RNNs are used for sequential input values such as time series, audio, video, speech, text, finance, and weather data. Examples of their uses in consumer products include Apple's Siri, Google's Translate, and Amazon's Alexa.

A schematic comparing traditional feed-forward networks with RNNs is as follows:

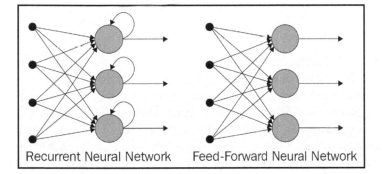

The loop back on each of the RNN units represents *memory*. Feed-forward networks have no way of distinguishing the order of items in a sequence, whereas RNNs depend fundamentally on the order of items. For example, suppose a feed-forward network received the input string *aardvark*: by the time the input is *d*, the network has forgotten that the previous input values were *a*, *a*, and *r*, so it is not possible for it to predict that *va* could be next. On the other hand, a recurrent network, given the same input, "remembers" that the previous input values were *a*, *a*, and *r*, so it *is* possible for it to predict that *va* could be next, depending upon its prior training.

The input to the network of each individual item to an RNN is known as a **time step**. So, for example, with a character-level RNN, the input of each character is a time step. The following diagram illustrates what is known as the *unrolling* of an RNN.

The time steps begin at $t = 0$, with an input of $\mathbf{X_0}$, and continue up to time step $t = t$ with input $\mathbf{X_t}$, and corresponding output values $\mathbf{h_0}$ to $\mathbf{h_t}$, as shown in the following diagram:

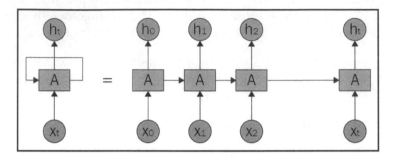

An unrolled recurrent neural network

RNNs are trained with backpropagation in a process known as **Backpropagation Through Time (BPTT)**. This is where it's useful to imagine that unfolding (also called **unrolling**) the RNN creates a sequence of neural networks and the error is calculated for each time step and combined so that the weights in the network can be updated as usual with backpropagation. For example, in order to calculate the gradient, and hence the error, at time step $t = 6$, we would have to backpropagate through five steps and sum up the gradients. There are problems with this approach, however, when trying to learn long-term dependencies (that is, between time steps that are far apart) because the gradients may become too small and make learning either impossible, or very slow, or they may become too big and swamp the network. This is known as the vanishing/exploding gradient problem, and various modifications have been invented to deal with it, including **Long Short Term Memory (LSTM)** networks and **Gated Recurrent Units (GRUs)**, which last we shall use later.

The following diagram shows more detail about unrolling (or unfolding):

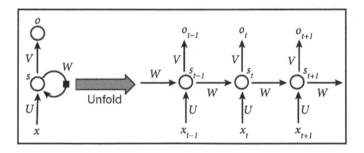

Schematic of a recurrent neural network

In the diagram, we can see the following:

- x_t is the input at time step **t**. For example, x_t could be the tenth character in a character-based RNN, represented as an index from the character set.
- s_t is the hidden state at the time step **t**, and as such, is the memory of the network.
- s_t is calculated as $s_t = f(Ux_t + Ws_{t-1})$, where f is a non-linear function such as ReLU. **U**, **V**, and **W** are the weights.
- o_t is the output at time step **t**. For example, if we wanted to calculate the next letter in a character sequence, it would be a vector of probabilities across the character set $o_t = Vs_t$.

As previously remarked, we can view s_t as the memory of the network, in that it contains information about what has happened at earlier time steps in the network. Notice that the weights **U**, **V**, and **W** are shared across every step because we are performing the same computation at every step, just with different input values (with the consequence that the number of weights to learn is significantly reduced). Notice also that we may not need output values at each time step (as shown in the diagram). If we were dealing with sentiment analysis, where each time step was a word in, say, the movie review, we would probably only care about the final output (positive or negative).

Let's now have a look at an interesting example of the use of an RNN where we try to create text in the style of a given piece of writing.

An application of RNNs

In this application, we will see how to create text using a character-based recurrent neural network. It is easy to change the corpus of text that to be used (see the example to follow); here, we will use the novel *Great Expectations* by Charles Dickens. We will train the network on this text so that, if we give it a character sequence such as *thousan*, it will produce the next character in the sequence, *d*. This process can be continued, and longer sequences of text created by calling the model repeatedly on the evolving sequence.

Here is an example of the text created before the model is trained:

```
Input:
 'o else is there to inform?"\n\n"Is there no chance person who might
identify you in the street?" said\n'
Next Char Predictions:
 "dUFdZ!mig())'(ZIon"4g&HZ"@\nWGWtlinnqQY*dGJ7ioU'6(vLKL&cJ29LG'1QW8n-
,M!JSVy"cjN;1cH\ndEEeMXhtW$U8Mt&sp"
```

And here is some text seeded with the `Pip` sequence created after the model has been trained for 100 epochs (at ~10s/epoch) with temperature (see later) of 0.1:

```
Pip; it was not to be done. I had been a little while I was a look out and
the strength of considerable particular by the windows of the rest of his
prospering look at the windows of the room wing and the courtyard in the
morning was the first time I had been a very much being strictly under the
wall of my own person to me that he had done my sister, and I went on with
the street common, I should have been a very little for an air of the river
by the fire. For the man who was all the time of the money. My dear
Herbert, who was a little way to the marshes he had ever seemed to have had
once more than once and the more was a ragged hand before I had ever seemed
to have him a dreadful loveriement in his head and with a falling to the
table, and I went on with his arms, I saw him ever so many times, and we
all the courtyard to the fire to be so often to be on some time when I saw
his shoulder as if it were a long time in the morning I was a woman and a
singer at the tide was remained by the
```

This isn't a bad result for a system that began with no knowledge of syntax or spelling. It's clearly nonsensical, but then we weren't aiming for sense. There is only one non-existent word (`loveriement`). So, the network has done its job of learning spelling and learning that words are units of text. Notice also, in the following code, that the network is trained on only short sequences (`sequence_length = 100`).

Next, we will look at the code for setting up, training, and testing the recurrent neural network.

The code for our RNN example

This application is based on one provided by Google under an Apache 2 license.

As usual, we will break the code down into snippets and refer you to the repository for the license and the full working version. Firstly, we have module imports, as follows:

```
import tensorflow as tf
import numpy as np
import os
import time
```

Next, we have the download link for the text file.

You can easily change this to any text you wish by specifying the file name in `file` and the full URL of the file in `url`:

```
file='1400-0.txt'
url='https://www.gutenberg.org/files/1400/1400-0.txt' # Great Expectations
by Charles Dickens
```

And then we set up the Keras `get_file()` utility for that file, shown as follows:

```
path = tf.keras.utils.get_file(file,url)
```

Then, we open and read the file and see how long it is, in characters:

```
text = open(path).read()
print ('Length of text: {} characters'.format(len(text)))
```

There is the text we don't need at the start of the file so we strip that off and then since it is instructive to look at the first few characters, we do that next:

```
# strip off text we don't need
text = text[835:]

# Take a look at the first 300 characters in text
print(text[:300])
```

The output should be as follows:

```
My father's family name being Pirrip, and my Christian name Philip, my
infant tongue could make of both names nothing longer or more explicit
than Pip. So, I called myself Pip, and came to be called Pip.

I give Pirrip as my father's family name, on the authority of his
tombstone and my sister,--Mrs
```

Let's now see how many unique characters there are in the text, using a set to get these, and sort them in order of their ASCII codes:

```
# The unique characters in the file
vocabulary = sorted(set(text))
print ('{} unique characters.'.format(len(vocabulary)))
```

This should give 84 unique characters.

Next, we create a dictionary where the characters are the keys, and successive integers are the values.

This is so we can find the index, meaning the numerical value for any given character:

```
# Create a  dictionary of unique character keys to index values
char_to_index = {char:index for index, char in enumerate(vocabulary)}
print(char_to_index)
```

The output is as follows:

```
{'\n': 0, ' ': 1, '!': 2, '$': 3, '%': 4, '&': 5, "'": 6, '(': 7, ')': 8,
'*': 9, ',': 10, '-': 11, '.': 12, '/': 13, '0': 14, '1': 15, '2': 16, '3':
17, '4': 18, '5': 19, '6': 20, '7': 21, '8': 22, '9': 23, ':': 24, ';': 25,
'?': 26, '@': 27, 'A': 28, 'B': 29, 'C': 30, 'D': 31, 'E': 32, 'F': 33,
'G': 34, 'H': 35, 'I': 36, 'J': 37, 'K': 38, 'L': 39, 'M': 40, 'N': 41,
'O': 42, 'P': 43, 'Q': 44, 'R': 45, 'S': 46, 'T': 47, 'U': 48, 'V': 49,
'W': 50, 'X': 51, 'Y': 52, 'Z': 53, 'a': 54, 'b': 55, 'c': 56, 'd': 57,
'e': 58, 'f': 59, 'g': 60, 'h': 61, 'i': 62, 'j': 63, 'k': 64, 'l': 65,
'm': 66, 'n': 67, 'o': 68, 'p': 69, 'q': 70, 'r': 71, 's': 72, 't': 73,
'u': 74, 'v': 75, 'w': 76, 'x': 77, 'y': 78, 'z': 79, 'ê': 80, 'ô': 81, '"':
82, '"': 83}
```

We will also need the characters to be stored in an array. This is so we can find the character corresponding to any given numerical value, that is, `index`:

```
index_to_char = np.array(vocabulary)
print(index_to_char)
```

The output is as follows:

```
['\n' ' ' '!' '$' '%' '&' "'" '(' ')' '*' ',' '-' '.' '/' '0' '1' '2' '3'
'4' '5' '6' '7' '8' '9' ':' ';' '?' '@' 'A' 'B' 'C' 'D' 'E' 'F' 'G' 'H' 'I'
'J' 'K' 'L' 'M' 'N' 'O' 'P' 'Q' 'R' 'S' 'T' 'U' 'V' 'W' 'X' 'Y' 'Z' 'a' 'b'
'c' 'd' 'e' 'f' 'g' 'h' 'i' 'j' 'k' 'l' 'm' 'n' 'o' 'p' 'q' 'r' 's' 't' 'u'
'v' 'w' 'x' 'y' 'z' 'ê' 'ô' '"' '"']
```

And now the entire text we are using has been translated into an array of the integers we created as a dictionary, `char_to_index`:

```
text_as_int = np.array([char_to_index[char] for char in text]
```

Here's a sample of the characters and their indices:

```
print('{')
for char,_ in zip(char_to_index, range(20)):
    print(' {:4s}: {:3d},'.format(repr(char), char_to_index[char]))
print(' ...\n}')
```

The output is as follows:

```
{
    '\n' :    0,
    ' '  :    1,
    '!'  :    2,
    '$'  :    3,
    '%'  :    4,
    '&'  :    5,
    '"'  :    6,
    '('  :    7,
    ')'  :    8,
    '*'  :    9,
    ','  :   10,
    '-'  :   11,
    '.'  :   12,
    '/'  :   13,
    '0'  :   14,
    '1'  :   15,
    '2'  :   16,
    '3'  :   17,
    '4'  :   18,
    '5'  :   19,
    ...
}
```

Next, it's useful to see how the text maps to integers; here are the first few:

```
# Show how the first 15 characters from the text are mapped to integers
print ('{} ---- characters mapped to int ---- > {}'.format(repr(text[:15]),
text_as_int[:15]))
```

The output is as follows:

```
"My father's fam" ---- characters mapped to int ---- > [40 78  1 59 54 73
61 58 71  6 72  1 59 54 66]
```

Then, we set the sentence length per input, and hence, the number of examples in an epoch of training:

```
# The maximum length sentence we want for a single input in characters
sequence_length = 100
examples_per_epoch = len(text)//seq_length
```

Next, we create `data.Dataset` to be used later in training:

```
# Create training examples / targets
char_dataset = tf.data.Dataset.from_tensor_slices(text_as_int)
# Display , sanity check
for char in char_dataset.take(5):
  print(index_to_char[char.numpy()])
```

The output is as follows:

```
M
y

f
a
```

We need to batch this data for feeding to our RNN, so we do this next:

```
sequences = char_dataset.batch(sequence_length+1, drop_remainder=True)
```

Remember we have set `sequence_length = 100`, so the number of characters in a batch is 101.

Now we have a function to create our input data and target data (required output).

The function returns the text that we have been working with, together with the same text, but shifted one character along, that is, if the first word is `Python` and `sequence_length = 5`, the function returns `Pytho` and `ython`.

We then create our dataset by joining the input and output character sequences:

```
def split_input_target(chunk):
    input_text = chunk[:-1]
    target_text = chunk[1:]
    return input_text, target_text

dataset = sequences.map(split_input_target)
```

Next, we perform another sanity check. We use the dataset created previously to display the input and target data.

Note that the `dataset.take(n)` method returns n batches from the dataset.

Note also here that, since we have eager execution enabled (by default, of course, in TensorFlow 2), we can use the `numpy()` method to find the value of a tensor:

```
for input_example, target_example in dataset.take(1):
 print ('Input data: ',
repr(''.join(index_to_char[input_example.numpy()]))) #101 characters
 print ('Target data:',
repr(''.join(index_to_char[target_example.numpy()])))
```

The output is as follows:

```
Input data: "My father's family name being Pirrip, and my Christian name
Philip, my\ninfant tongue could make of b" Target data: "y father's family
name being Pirrip, and my Christian name Philip, my\ninfant tongue could
make of bo"
```

We can now show the input and expected output for a few steps:

```
for char, (input_index, target_index) in enumerate(zip(input_example[:5],
target_example[:5])):
    print("Step {:4d}".format(char))
    print(" input: {} ({:s})".format(input_index,
repr(index_to_char[input_index])))
    print(" expected output: {} ({:s})".format(target_index,
repr(index_to_char[target_index])))
```

The following is the output of this:

```
Step 0:       input: 40 ('M'),  expected output: 78 ('y')
Step 1:       input: 78 ('y'),  expected output: 1 (' ')
Step 2:       input: 1 (' '),  expected output: 59 ('f')
Step 3:       input: 59 ('f'),  expected output: 54 ('a')
Step 4:       input: 54 ('a'),  expected output: 73 ('t')
```

Next, we set things up for training, as follows:

```
# how many characters in a batch
batch = 64

# the number of training steps taken in each epoch
steps_per_epoch = examples_per_epoch//batch # note integer division

# TF data maintains a buffer in memory in which to shuffle data
# since it is designed to work with possibly endless data
buffer = 10000

dataset = dataset.shuffle(buffer).batch(batch, drop_remainder=True)
```

```
# call repeat() on dataset so data can be re-fed into the model from the
beginning
dataset = dataset.repeat()

dataset
```

This gives the following dataset structure:

**`<RepeatBatchDataset shapes: ((64, 100), (64, 100)), types: (tf.int64,
tf.int64)>`**

Here, 64 is the batch size and 100 is the sequence length. The following are some values we need for the training:

```
# The vocabulary length in characters
vocabulary_length = len(vocabulary)

# The embedding dimension
embedding_dimension = 256

# The number of recurrent neural network units
recurrent_nn_units = 1024
```

We are using GRUs, and within **CUDA Deep Neural Network (cuDNN)** library, there are fast routines for these computations that we can use if our code is running on a GPU. GRUs are a way of implementing memory in an RNN. The next section implements this idea, shown as follows:

```
if tf.test.is_gpu_available():
    recurrent_nn = tf.compat.v1.keras.layers.CuDNNGRU
    print("GPU in use")
else:
    import functools
    recurrent_nn = functools.partial(tf.keras.layers.GRU,
recurrent_activation='sigmoid')
    print("CPU in use")
```

Building and instantiating our model

As we have seen previously, one technique for building a model is to pass the required layers into the `tf.keras.Sequential()` constructor. In this instance, we have three layers: an embedding layer, an RNN layer, and a dense layer.

The first, embedding layer is a lookup table of vectors, one vector for the numeric value of each character. It has the dimension, `embedding_dimension`. The middle, the recurrent layer is a GRU; its size is `recurrent_nn_units`. The last layer is a dense output layer of the length `vocabulary_length` units.

What the model does is look up the embedding, run the GRU for a single time step using the embedding for input, and pass this to the dense layer, which generates logits (log odds) for the next character.

A diagram showing this is as follows:

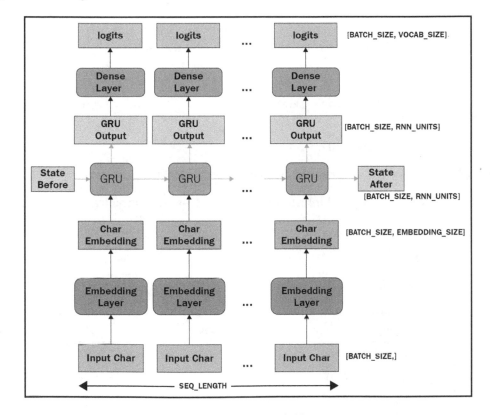

The code that implements this model is, therefore, as follows:

```
def build_model(vocabulary_size, embedding_dimension, recurrent_nn_units,
batch_size):
    model = tf.keras.Sequential(
        [tf.keras.layers.Embedding(vocabulary_size, embedding_dimension,
batch_input_shape=[batch_size, None]),
    recurrent_nn(recurrent_nn_units, return_sequences=True,
```

```
    recurrent_initializer='glorot_uniform', stateful=True),
        tf.keras.layers.Dense(vocabulary_length)
    ])
        return model
```

Now we can instantiate our model as follows:

```
model = build_model(
    vocabulary_size = len(vocabulary),
    embedding_dimension=embedding_dimension,
    recurrent_nn_units=recurrent_nn_units,
    batch_size=batch)
```

We can now run a sanity check to make sure our model outputs the correct shapes. Notice the use of `dataset.take()` to extract an element of the dataset:

```
for batch_input_example, batch_target_example in dataset.take(1):
    batch_predictions_example = model(batch_input_example)
    print(batch_predictions_example.shape, "# (batch, sequence_length,
vocabulary_length)")
```

The following is the output of this:

(64, 100, 84) # (batch, sequence_length, vocabulary_length)

This is as expected; recall we had 84 unique characters in our character set.

And here is the code to show what our model looks like:

```
model.summary()
```

The output of our model architecture summary is as follows:

```
Layer (type)                 Output Shape              Param #
=================================================================
embedding (Embedding)        (64, None, 256)           21504

cu_dnngru (CuDNNGRU)         (64, None, 1024)          3938304

dense (Dense)                (64, None, 84)            86100
=================================================================
Total params: 4,045,908
Trainable params: 4,045,908
Non-trainable params: 0
```

Recalling again that we have 84 input values, we can see that, for the embedding layer, *84*256 = 21,504*, and for the dense layer, *1024*84 +84 (bias units) = 86,100*.

Using our model to get predictions

To get the predictions from our model, we need to take a sample from the output distribution. This sampling will get us the characters we need from that output distribution (sampling the output distribution is important because taking the `argmax` of it, as we would normally do, can easily get the model stuck in a loop).

`tf.random.categorical` does this sampling and `tf.squeeze` with `axis=-1` removes the last dimension of the tensor, prior to displaying the indices.

The signature of `tf.random.categorical` is as follows:

```
tf.random.categorical(logits, num_samples, seed=None, name=None,
output_dtype=None)
```

Comparing this with the call, we see that we are taking one sample (of length `sequence_length = 100`) from the predictions (`example_batch_predictions[0]`). The extra dimension is then removed, so we can look up the characters corresponding to the sample:

```
sampled_indices =
tf.random.categorical(logits=batch_predictions_example[0], num_samples=1)

sampled_indices = tf.squeeze(sampled_indices,axis=-1).numpy()

sampled_indices
```

This produces the following output:

```
array([79, 43, 3, 12, 20, 24, 54, 10, 61, 43, 46, 15, 0, 24, 39, 77, 2, 73,
4, 78, 5, 60, 13, 65, 1, 75, 47, 33, 61, 13, 64, 41, 32, 42, 40, 20, 37,
10, 60, 51, 21, 17, 69, 8, 3, 74, 64, 68, 2, 3, 35, 13, 67, 16, 46, 48, 47,
1, 38, 80, 47, 8, 32, 53, 50, 28, 63, 33, 35, 72, 80, 0, 7, 64, 2, 79, 1,
56, 61, 13, 55, 28, 62, 30, 40, 22, 32, 40, 27, 46, 21, 51, 10, 76, 64, 47,
72, 83, 45, 8])
```

Let's take a look at some input and output *prior* to training:

```
print("Input: \n", repr("".join(index_to_char[batch_input_example[0]])))

print("Next Char Predictions: \n",
repr("".join(index_to_char[sampled_indices ])))
#
```

So the output is as follows. The input text is followed by the next character predictions (before training):

```
Input:
 'r, that I might refer to it again; but I could not find it, and\nwas
uneasy to think that it must hav'
Next Char Predictions:
"hFTzJe;rAô:G*'"x4d?&ôce9QekL:*O7@KuoZM&"$r0mg\n%/2-6QaE&$)/'Y8m.x)94b?fKp.r
Rô.3IMMTMjMMag.iL1LuM6 ?';"
```

Next, we define our `loss` function:

```
def loss(labels, logits):
  return tf.keras.losses.sparse_categorical_crossentropy(labels, logits,
from_logits=True)
```

Then, we look at our model's loss before training and do another size sanity check:

```
batch_loss_example =
tf.compat.v1.losses.sparse_softmax_cross_entropy(batch_target_example,
batch_predictions_example)
print("Prediction shape: ", batch_predictions_example.shape, " #
(batch_size, sequence_length, vocab_size)")
print("scalar_loss: ", batch_loss_example.numpy())
```

This produces the following output:

```
Prediction shape: (64, 100, 84) # (batch, sequence_length,
vocabulary_length)
scalar_loss: 4.429237
```

To prepare our model for training, we now compile it with `AdamOptimizer` and a softmax cross entropy loss:

```
#next produced by upgrade script....
#model.compile(optimizer = tf.compat.v1.train.AdamOptimizer(), loss = loss)
#.... but following optimizer is available.
model.compile(optimizer = tf.optimizers.Adam(), loss = loss)
```

We are going to save the model's weights, so next, we prepare the checkpoints for this:

```
# The checkpoints will be saved in this directory
directory = './checkpoints'

# checkpoint files
file_prefix = os.path.join(directory, "ckpt_{epoch}")
callback=[tf.keras.callbacks.ModelCheckpoint(filepath=file_prefix,
save_weights_only=True)]
```

And finally, we can train our model using a call to `model.fit()`:

```
epochs=45 # *much* faster on GPU, ~10s / epoch, reduce this figure
significantly if on CPU

history = model.fit(dataset, epochs=epochs,
steps_per_epoch=steps_per_epoch, callbacks=callback)
```

This gives the following output:

```
Epoch 1/50 158/158 [==============================] - 10s 64ms/step - loss:
2.6995
..................
Epoch 50/50 158/158 [==============================] - 10s 65ms/step -
loss: 0.6143
```

The following is the most recent checkpoint:

```
tf.train.latest_checkpoint(directory)
```

This resolves to the following result:

```
'./checkpoints/ckpt_45'
```

So we can rebuild our model (to show how it's done):

```
model = build_model(vocabulary_size, embedding_dimension,
recurrent_nn_units, batch_size=1)

model.load_weights(tf.train.latest_checkpoint(directory))

model.build(tf.TensorShape([1, None]))

model.summary()
```

So the summary for our model is shown in the following table:

```
Layer (type)                 Output Shape              Param #
=================================================================
embedding_1 (Embedding)      (1, None, 256)            21504

cu_dnngru_1 (CuDNNGRU)       (1, None, 1024)           3938304

dense_1 (Dense)              (1, None, 84)             86100
=================================================================
Total params: 4,045,908
Trainable params: 4,045,908
Non-trainable params: 0
```

Next, we use a function to generate the new text, given our trained model, a start string, and temperature, the value of which determines how random the text is (low values give more predictable text; high values give more random text).

Firstly, we establish the number of characters to generate, then we vectorize our start string, adding a blank dimension to it. We add the extra dimension to our `input_string` variable because it is required by the RNN units (the two required dimensions being the batch length and sequence length). We then initialize a variable in which to store our generated text.

The value of `temperature` determines how random the generated text is (lower is less random, meaning more predictable).

Inside a loop with an iteration for each new character we want to generate, we use the model, which contains the RNN state, to get the prediction distribution of the next character. A multinomial distribution is then used to find the index of the predicted character, which is then used as our next input to the model. Due to the loop, the RNN state, returned by the model, is fed back into the model, so it now has more information than just one character. Once the next character has been predicted, the modified RNN states are repeatedly fed back into the model, so that the model learns, as the context it gets from previously predicted characters increases.

The following diagram shows how this works:

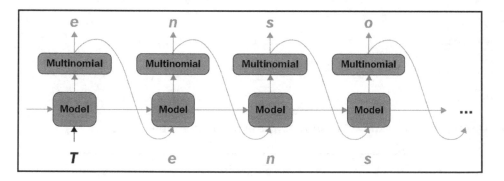

Here, the multinomial is implemented with `tf.random.categorical`; so we are now ready to generate our predicted text:

```python
def generate_text(model, start_string, temperature,
characters_to_generate):

# Vectorise the start string into numbers
  input_string = [char_to_index[char] for char in start_string]
# add extra dimension to input_string
  input_string = tf.expand_dims(input_string, 0)

# Empty list to store generated text
  generated = []

# (batch size is 1)
  model.reset_states()
  for i in range(characters_to_generate):
    predictions = model(input_string) #here's where we need the extra
dimension

    # remove the batch dimension
    predictions = tf.squeeze(predictions, 0)

    # using a random categorical (multinomial) distribution to predict word
returned by the model
    predictions = predictions / temperature
    predicted_id = tf.random.categorical(logits=predictions,
num_samples=1)[-1,0].numpy()

    # Pass  predicted word as  next input to the model along with previous
hidden state
    input_string = tf.expand_dims([predicted_id], 0)

    generated.append(index_to_char[predicted_id])
return (start_string + ''.join(generated)) # generated is a list
```

So, after defining our function, we can call it to return our generated text.

In the given arguments to the function, a low temperature gives more predictable text, whereas a high temperature gives more random text. Also, this is where you can change the start string and change the number of characters that the function generates:

```
generated_text = generate_text(model=model, start_string="Pip",
temperature=0.1, characters_to_generate = 1000)
print(generated_text)
```

This produces the following output after 30 epochs of training:

> Pip; it was a much better to and the Aged and weaking his hands of the
> windows of the way who went them on which the more I had been a very little
> for me, and I went on with his back in the soldiers of the room with the
> whole hand the other gentleman with the hand on the service, when I was a
> look of half of the room was was the first time of the money. I forgetter,
> Mr. Pip?" "I don't know that I have no more than I know what I have no
> inquiry with the rest of its being straight up again. He came out of the
> room, and in the midst of the room was was all the words, "and he came into
> the Castle. One would repeat it to your expectations condition of the
> courtyard. In a moment was the first time in the house to the fork, and we
> all lighted and at his being so beautiful looking at the convicts. My
> depression of the morning, I looked at him in the morning, I should not
> have been made a strong for the first time of the wall before the table to
> the forefinger of the room, and had not quite diffi

`Loss = 0.6761`; this text is more or less correctly spelled and punctuated, albeit its meaning (which we weren't trying to achieve) is pretty much gobbledygook. It hasn't learned how to use speech marks properly. There are only two nonsensical words, (`forgetter` and `weaking`) which, upon examination, are nevertheless semantically plausible. Whether or not the generated is in the style of Charles Dickens is an open question.

Experiments with the number of epochs reveal that the loss reaches a minimum at around 45 epochs, after which it starts to increase.

After 45 epochs the output is as follows:

```
Pip; or I should
have felt painfully consciousness that he was the man with his back to the
kitchen, and he seemed to have no
strength, and as I had often seen her shutters with the poker on
the parlor, through having been every disagreeable to be seen; I thought I
would give him more letters of my own
eyes and flared about the fire, and showed the greatest state of mind,
I thought I would give up of his having fastened out of the room, and had
made some advance in that respect to me to feel an
indescribable awe as it was a to be even than ever of her steps, or for old
asked, "Yes."

"What is it?" repeated Mr. Jaggers. "You know I was in my mind by his blue
eyes most of all admirers,
and that she had shaken hands contributing the poker out of his
hands in his pockets and his dinner loosely tied in a busy preparation for
the reference to my United and
self-possession when Miss Havisham and Estella now that I had been too much
to be the salvey dark night, which seemed so long
ago. "Yes, de
```

`Loss = 0.6166`; the model now seems to have paired up speech marks correctly, and there are no nonsensical words.

Summary

This concludes our look at RNNs. In this chapter, we first discussed the general principles of RNNs, and then saw how to acquire and prepare some text for use by a model, noting that it is straightforward to use an alternative source of text here. We then saw how to create and instantiate our model. We then trained our model and used it produce text from our starting string, noting that the network has learned that words are units of text and how to spell quite a variety of words, somewhat in the style of the author of the text, with only a couple of non-words.

In the next chapter, we will look at the use of TensorFlow Hub, which is a software library.

9
TensorFlow Estimators and TensorFlow Hub

This chapter is divided into two sections, but the technologies here are related. First, we will look at how TensorFlow Estimators provide a simple, high-level API for TensorFlow, and secondly, we will look at how TensorFlow Hub contains modules that we can make use of in our own applications.

In this chapter, we will cover the following main topics:

- TensorFlow Estimators
- TensorFlow Hub

TensorFlow Estimators

`tf.estimator` is a high-level API for TensorFlow. It is used to simplify machine learning programming by providing the means for the straightforward training, evaluation, predicting, and exporting of models for serving.

Estimators confer many advantages on the TensorFlow developer. It is easier and more intuitive to develop models with Estimators than with low-level APIs. In particular, the same model can be run on a local machine or on a distributed multi-server system. The model is also agnostic to the processor it finds itself on, that is, either CPUs, GPUs, or TPUs. Estimators also simplify the development process by making it easier for model developers to share implementations and, being built on Keras layers, make customization simpler.

Estimators take care of all of the background plumbing that goes into working with a TensorFlow model. They support safe, distributed training loops for graph building, for the initialization of variables, loading of data, handling of exceptions, creation of checkpoint files, recovery from failures, and saving of summaries for TensorBoard. As we shall see, since they create checkpoints, they support stopping and starting training after a given number of steps.

There are four steps in developing an Estimator model:

1. Acquire the data and create the data functions
2. Create the feature column(s)
3. Instantiate the Estimator
4. Evaluate the model's performance

We will exemplify these steps in the following code.

We have seen the `fashion_mnist` dataset before (in `Chapter 5`, *Unsupervised Learning Using TensorFlow 2*), so we will use this dataset again to demonstrate a use case for Estimators.

The code

First, here are the required imports:

```
import tensorflow as tf
import numpy as np
```

Next, we acquire and preprocess the data. Notice that `fashion_mnist` is handily present in `tf.keras.datasets`. The x values in the dataset are in the form of integer NumPy arrays, each element being in the range 0 to 255, representing the grayscale value at each of the pixels in the 28 x 28 pixels fashion image. For training purposes, these values must be converted into floats in the range of 0 to 1. The y values are in the form of unsigned 8-bit integers (`uint8`) and must be converted into 32-bit integers (`int32`), again for use by the Estimator.

The learning rate is set to quite a small value, although this hyperparameter value may be experimented with:

```
fashion = tf.keras.datasets.fashion_mnist
(x_train, y_train),(x_test, y_test) = fashion.load_data()
print(type(x_train))
x_train, x_test = x_train / 255.0, x_test / 255.0
```

```
y_train, y_test = np.int32(y_train), np.int32(y_test)

learning_rate = 1e-4
```

After that, comes our training input function.

`tf.compat.v1.estimator.inputs.numpy_input_fn` is used when you have the full dataset available in an array and want a quick way to do batching, shuffling, and/or repeating.

Its signature is as follows:

```
tf.compat.v1.estimator.inputs.numpy_input_fn(
  x,
  y=None,
  batch_size=128,
  num_epochs=1,
  shuffle=None,
  queue_capacity=1000,
  num_threads=1
)
```

Comparing this with our call of the function, you can see how the x values are passed in as a dictionary of NumPy arrays (compatible with tensors) and that y is passed in as is. At this stage, we are not specifying the number of epochs, that is, the function will run forever (steps will be specified later), our batch size, that is, the number of images presented in one step, is 50, and the data is shuffled in the queue before each step. Other arguments are left at their default values:

```
train_input_fn = tf.compat.v1.estimator.inputs.numpy_input_fn(
    x={"x": x_train},
        y=y_train,
        num_epochs=None,
        batch_size=50,
        shuffle=True
)
```

It is worth noting that such convenience functions, while not available in TensorFlow 2.0 alpha, are nevertheless expected to move to TensorFlow2 proper.

The testing function has the same signature but, in this case, we specify just one epoch and, as advised by Google, we do not shuffle the data. Again, the remaining arguments are left at their default values:

```
test_input_fn = tf.compat.v1.estimator.inputs.numpy_input_fn(
    x={"x": x_test},
        y=y_test,
```

```
        num_epochs=1,
        shuffle=False
)
```

Next, we establish our feature columns. Feature columns are a means of passing data to an Estimator.

The signature of the feature column function is as follows. `key` is a unique string, being the name of the column corresponding to the name of the dictionary we previously specified in our input function (further details about the different type of feature columns may be found at `https://www.tensorflow.org/api_docs/python/tf/feature_column`):

```
tf.feature_column.numeric_column(
    key,
    shape=(1,),
    default_value=None,
    dtype=tf.float32,
    normalizer_fn=None
)
```

In our specific feature column, we can see that the key is `"x"` and that the shape is what we know to be the 28 x 28 pixels shape of the `fashion_mnist` dataset images:

```
feature_columns = [tf.feature_column.numeric_column("x", shape=[28, 28])]
```

Next, we instantiate our Estimator, which will do the classification. It will construct a deep neural network for us. Its signature is very long and detailed, so we will refer you to `https://www.tensorflow.org/api_docs/python/tf/estimator/DNNClassifier` since we will mostly use its default arguments. Its first argument is the feature we just specified, while the second argument is our network size. (The input layer and the output layer are added in the background by the Estimator.) `AdamOptimizer` is a safe choice. `n_classes` corresponds to the number of `y` labels for our `fashion_mnist` dataset, which we add a modest `dropout` of `0.1`. Then, `model_dir` is the directory that we save the model parameters in, as well as its graph and checkpoints. This directory is also used to reload checkpoints into an Estimator to continue with the training:

```
# Build 2 layer DNN classifier
classifier = tf.estimator.DNNClassifier(
    feature_columns=feature_columns,
    hidden_units=[256, 32],
    optimizer=tf.compat.v1.train.AdamOptimizer(learning_rate),
    n_classes=10,
    dropout=0.1,
    model_dir="./tmp/mnist_modelx"
, loss_reduction=tf.compat.v1.losses.Reduction.SUM)
```

Now, we are ready to train our model. If you run the `.train` loop a second or subsequent times, then the Estimator will load its model parameters from `model_dir` and carry on training for further `steps` (to start completely from scratch, you just need to delete the directory specified by `model_dir`):

```
classifier.train(input_fn=train_input_fn, steps=10000)
```

A typical output line looks as follows:

```
INFO:tensorflow:loss = 25.540459, step = 1600 (0.179 sec)
INFO:tensorflow:global_step/sec: 523.471
```

The final output looks as follows:

```
INFO:tensorflow:Saving checkpoints for 10000 into
./tmp/mnist_modelx/model.ckpt.
INFO:tensorflow:Loss for final step: 13.06977.
```

The directory specified in `model_dir` looks as follows:

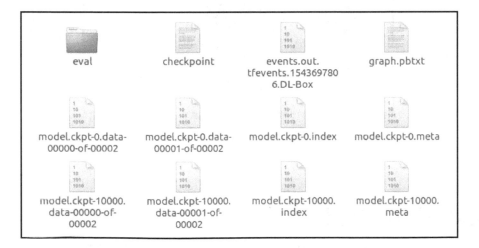

To evaluate the performance of the model, the `classifier.evaluate` method is used. Its signature is as follows:

```
classifier.evaluate(input_fn, steps=None, hooks=None, checkpoint_path=None,
name=None)
```

This returns a dictionary, so in our call, we are extracting the accuracy metric.

Here, `steps` defaults to `None`. This evaluates the model until `input_fn` raises an end-of-input exception, that is, it evaluates on the entire test set:

```
accuracy_score = classifier.evaluate(input_fn=test_input_fn)["accuracy"]
print("\nTest Accuracy: {0:f}%\n".format(accuracy_score*100))
```

We can also see the progress of the training in TensorBoard with the following command:

```
tensorboard --logdir=./tmp/mnist_modelx
```

Here, the loss graph looks as follows, where the *x*-axis is in 1,000 (k) units:

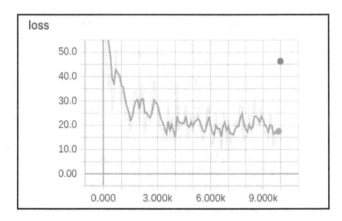

This concludes our look at the fashion Estimator classifier. We will now look at TensorFlow Hub.

TensorFlow Hub

TensorFlow Hub is a software library. Its purpose is to provide reusable components, known as modules, that can be leveraged in contexts other than the original context in which they were developed. By a module, we mean a self-contained piece of a TensorFlow graph, along with its weights, which can be reused across other, similar tasks.

IMDb (database of movie reviews)

In this section, we will examine an application based on one from Google that analyzes a subset of the IMDb of movie reviews in what is termed **sentiment analysis**. The subset is hosted by Stanford and contains reviews of each movie, together with a sentiment on a positivity scale of 1 to 4 (bad) and 7 to 10 (good). The problem is determining the polarity of the view expressed in a sentence of text about each movie, that is, for each review, to determine whether it is a positive or a negative review. We will make use of a module in TensorFlow Hub that has previously been trained to produce word embeddings.

A word embedding is a vector of numbers so that words with a similar meaning have a similar vector. This is an example of supervised learning because the training set of reviews will use the value of positivity, as supplied by the IMDB database, to train a model. We will then use the trained model on the test set and see how its predictions compare with those stored in the IMDB database to give us an accuracy measure.

The citation for the database paper can be found at `http://ai.stanford.edu/~amaas/data/sentiment/`.

The dataset

The following is from the README that accompanies the database (`http://ai.stanford.edu/~amaas/data/sentiment/`):

> *"The core dataset contains 50,000 reviews split evenly into 25k train and 25k test sets. The overall distribution of labels is balanced (25k pos and 25k neg)."*
> *"In the entire collection, no more than 30 reviews are allowed for any given movie because reviews for the same movie tend to have correlated ratings. Further, the train and test sets contain a disjoint set of movies, so no significant performance is obtained by memorizing movie-unique terms and their associated with observed labels. In the labeled train/test sets, a negative review has a score <= 4 out of 10, and a positive review has a score >= 7 out of 10. Thus, reviews with more neutral ratings are not included in the train/test sets."*

Here is an example of five rows from the head of the IMDb train set:

	Sentence	Sentiment	Polarity
0	I came here for a review last night before dec...	3	0
1	Look, I'm reading and reading these comments and...	4	0
2	I was overtaken by the emotion. Unforgettable ...	10	1
3	This movie could have been a decent B-movie if...	4	0
4	I have a thing for old black and white movies ...	10	1

Here are five rows from its tail:

	Sentence	Sentiment	Polarity
24995	I have watched some pretty poor films in the p...	1	0
24996	This film is a calculated attempt to cash in t...	1	0
24997	This movie was so very badly written. The char...	1	0
24998	I am a huge Stooges fan but the one and only r...	2	0
24999	Well, let me start off by saying how utterly H...	3	0

The following is from the test set:

```
train_df.head()
```

	description	sentiment	polarity
0	I have to admit, I wasn't expecting much going...	9	1
1	Of the three titles from Jess Franco to find t...	3	0
2	This movie wasn't just bad - it was terrible. ...	1	0
3	I love this film 'Spring and port wine'. I was...	10	1
4	Not being familiar with US television stations...	4	0

```
train_df.tail()
```

	description	sentiment	polarity
24995	You know a movie will not go well when John Ca...	1	0
24996	The story centers around Barry McKenzie who mu...	10	1
24997	I'm not a writer or an critic...I'M just a stu...	10	1
24998	Jake's Closet has the emotional power of Krame...	9	1
24999	This wretched movie shows that not even some o...	2	0

The code

Now, let's look at the code that trains on this data. At the top of the program, we have our usual imports, together with three extra ones that may need installing with `pip` – `tensorflow_hub`, `pandas`, and `seaborn`. As we mentioned previously, we will be using a module from `tensorflow_hub`; we will also be using some DataFrame properties of `pandas` and some plotting methods of `seaborn`:

```
import tensorflow as tf
import tensorflow_hub as hub
import matplotlib.pyplot as plt
import numpy as np
import os
import pandas as pd
import re
import seaborn as sns
```

Also, here are some values and a method we need later:

```
n_classes = 2
hidden_units = [500,100]
learning_rate = 1e-4
steps = 1000
optimizer = tf.optimizers.Adagrad(learning_rate=learning_rate)
# upgrade script gave this:
#optimizer = tf.compat.v1.train.AdagradOptimizer(learning_rate =
learning_rate)
```

It is important to realize that the IMDb data that's used here is in the form of a hierarchical structure of directories.

The top-level IMDb directory contains two sub-directories: `train` and `test`. The `train` and `test` sub-directories each contain two further sub-directories, `pos` and `neg`:

- `pos`: This contains a collection of text files. Each text file is a positive review (polarity of 1).
- `neg`: This contains a collection of text files. Each text file is a negative review (polarity of 0).

The sentiment (7 to 10 or 1 to 4, respectively) is captured in the filename; for example, the text file review with a filename of 18_7.txt has a sentiment of 7 (pos), while the text file review with a filename of 38_2.txt has a sentiment of 2 (neg):

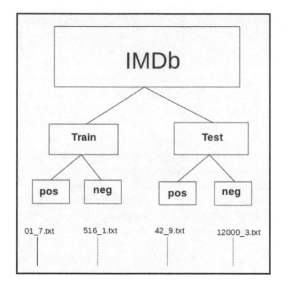

The IMDb directory/file hierarchy

We start with three functions in a call hierarchy that acquire and preprocess the review data.

In the first function, load_data(directory), directory_data is a dictionary that is loaded with data from directory, which is passed in as an argument and returned as a pandas DataFrame.

The directory_data dictionary is initialized with the description and sentiment keys, which are then assigned empty lists as values.

The function then loops over each file in directory and, for each text file, reads and appends its contents (being a movie review) to the sentiment list. It then analyzes the filename with a regular expression and extracts the numerical sentiment, which, as shown previously, follows the underscore (_) in the filename. The function appends this numerical sentiment to the sentiment list. When all of the .txt files have been looped through, the function returns the dictionary that was cast into a pandas DataFrame:

```
# Load all files from a directory into a Pandas DataFrame.
def load_data(directory):
    directory_data = {}
```

```
        directory_data["description"] = []
        directory_data["sentiment"] = []
        for file in os.listdir(directory):
            with tf.io.gfile.GFile(os.path.join(directory, file), "r") as f:
                directory_data["description"].append(f.read())
                directory_data["sentiment"].append(re.match("\d+_(\d+)\.txt",
file).group(1))
        return pd.DataFrame.from_dict(directory_data)
```

The next function, `load(directory)`, calls `load_data(directory)`, as we described previously, to create a DataFrame from the `pos` and `neg` sub-directories. It adds the appropriate polarity as an extra field to each DataFrame. It then returns a new DataFrame that consists of a concatenation of `pos` and `neg` DataFrames, shuffled (`sample(frac=1)`) with a new numerical index inserted (since we have shuffled the rows):

```
# Merge positive and negative examples, add a polarity column and shuffle.
def load(directory):
    positive_df = load_data(os.path.join(directory, "pos"))
    positive_df["polarity"] = 1

    negative_df = load_data(os.path.join(directory, "neg"))
    negative_df["polarity"] = 0
    return pd.concat([positive_df,
negative_df]).sample(frac=1).reset_index(drop=True)
```

The third and final function is `acquire_data()`. This function uses a Keras utility to get the file we require from the Stanford URL if it is not already present in the cache. The cache is the directory located at `~/.keras/datasets` by default, and the file is extracted to this location if necessary. The utility returns the path to our IMDb. This is then passed to two calls of `load_dataset()` for the acquisition of the train and test DataFrames:

```
# Download and process the dataset files.
def acquire_data():
    data = tf.keras.utils.get_file(
    fname="aclImdb.tar.gz",
origin="http://ai.stanford.edu/~amaas/data/sentiment/aclImdb_v1.tar.gz",
extract=True)

    train_df = load(os.path.join(os.path.dirname(data), "aclImdb",
"train"))
    test_df = load(os.path.join(os.path.dirname(data), "aclImdb", "test"))

    return train_df, test_df
tf.compat.v1.logging.set_verbosity(tf.compat.v1.logging.ERROR)
```

The first thing the main program does is acquire the train and test pandas DataFrames with a call to the function we just described:

```
train_df, test_df = acquire_data()
```

At this point, `train_df` and `test_df` contain the data we are going to work with.

Before we look at the next snippet, let's see its signature. This is an Estimator that returns an input function for feeding the Pandas DataFrame into the model:

```
tf.compat.v1.estimator.inputs.pandas_input_fn(x, y=None, batch_size=128,
num_epochs=1, shuffle=None, queue_capacity=1000, num_threads=1,
target_column='target')
```

The call itself is as follows:

```
# Training input on the whole training set with no limit on training epochs
train_input_fn = tf.compat.v1.estimator.inputs.pandas_input_fn(train_df,
train_df["polarity"], num_epochs=None, shuffle=True)
```

By comparing this call with the function signature, we can see that the training DataFrame, `train_df`, is passed in together with the polarity of each review. `num_epochs =None` indicates that there is no limit on the number of training epochs since we will specify this later, and `shuffle=True` indicates that the records, that is, each line of the file, are read in random order.

Next comes the function for predicting the result of training:

```
# Prediction on the whole training set.
predict_train_input_fn =
tf.compat.v1.estimator.inputs.pandas_input_fn(train_df,
train_df["polarity"], shuffle=False)
```

We also have the function for predicting the result of testing:

```
# Prediction on the test set.
predict_test_input_fn =
tf.compat.v1.estimator.inputs.pandas_input_fn(test_df, test_df["polarity"],
shuffle=False)
```

Then, we have our feature column. A feature column is an intermediary between raw data and an Estimator. There are nine feature column types altogether. They take either numerical or categorical data, depending on their type, and transform data into a format that's suitable for an Estimator. There is an excellent description, together with lots of examples, at `https://www.tensorflow.org/guide/feature_columns`.

Notice that the embedding comes from `tf.hub`:

```
embedded_text_feature_column = hub.text_embedding_column(
    key="description",
    module_spec="https://tfhub.dev/google/nnlm-en-dim128/1")
```

Next, we have our deep neural network Estimator. An Estimator is a high-level tool for working with models.

Examples of Estimators include `DNNClassifier`, that is, a classifier for TensorFlow deep neural networks (as used in the following code), and `LinearRegressor`, that is, a classifier for linear regression problem. Its signature is as follows:

```
tf.estimator.DNNClassifier(hidden_units, feature_columns, model_dir=None,
n_classes=2, weight_column=None, label_vocabulary=None,
optimizer='Adagrad', activation_fn=<function relu at 0x7fbb75512488>,
dropout=None, input_layer_partitioner=None, config=None,
warm_start_from=None, loss_reduction='weighted_sum', batch_norm=False,
loss_reduction=None)
```

Let's compare this to the call:

```
estimator = tf.estimator.DNNClassifier(
    hidden_units = hidden_units,
    feature_columns=[embedded_text_feature_column],
    n_classes=n_classes,
    optimizer= optimiser,
    model_dir = "./tmp/IMDbModel"
, loss_reduction=tf.compat.v1.losses.Reduction.SUM)
```

We can see that we are going to use a neural network with hidden layers of 500 and 100 units, our previously defined feature column, two output classes (labels), and a ProximalAdagrad optimizer.

Note that, as in the previous example, because we have specified `model_dir`, the Estimator will save a checkpoint and the various model parameters so that if the is training rerun, the model will be loaded from this directory and trained for further `steps`.

Now, we can train our network with the following code:

```
estimator.train(input_fn=train_input_fn, steps=steps);
```

This block of code creates a confusion matrix for our results.

A confusion matrix, in our context, is a diagram that shows the following for the trained model:

- **True positives**: Reviews whose true positive sentimentality has been correctly predicted as positive (bottom-right)
- **True negatives**: Reviews whose true negative sentimentality has been correctly predicted as negative (top-left)
- **False positives**: Reviews whose true negative sentimentality has been incorrectly predicted as positive (top-right)
- **False negatives**: Reviews whose true positive sentimentality has been incorrectly predicted as negative (bottom-left)

The following is the confusion matrix for our training set:

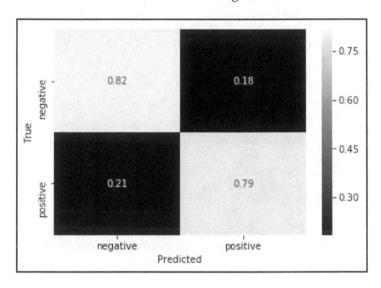

The confusion matrix for the training set

The raw figures are as follows:

9,898	2602
2,314	10,186

Notice how the total is 25,000, which is the number of training examples we used.

Here is the confusion matrix for our test set:

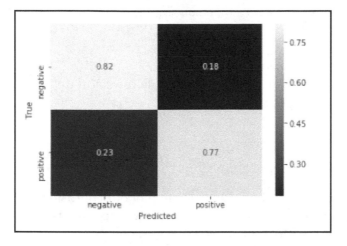

The confusion matrix for the test set

The raw figures are as follows:

9859	2641
2500	10000

With a confusion matrix, it is important that the values on the leading diagonal (top-left to bottom-right) are much higher than the value of this diagonal; we can see immediately from our confusion matrices that our model has performed well on both the train and the test set (if a little worse on the test set).

In the code, we first have a function to get predictions:

```
def get_predictions(estimator, input_fn):
    return [prediction["class_ids"][0] for prediction in
estimator.predict(input_fn=input_fn)]
```

TensorFlow has a method to create confusion matrices (so that they appear in the raw figures, as described previously).

Its signature is as follows:

```
tf.math.confusion_matrix(labels, predictions, num_classes=None,
dtype=tf.int32, name=None, weights=None)
```

Here, `labels` are the true labels.

Our code calls the method like this:

```
confusion_train = tf.math.confusion_matrix(labels=train_df["polarity"],
predictions=get_predictions(estimator, predict_train_input_fn))
print("Raw figures:")
print(confusion_train.numpy())
```

Next, we normalize the confusion matrix so that its rows add up to 1:

```
# Normalize the confusion matrix so that each row sums to 1.

top = confusion_train.numpy()
bottom = np.sum(top)
confusion_train = 2*top/bottom
```

Finally, we use a `seaborn` method, `heatmap`, to plot our confusion matrix. The signature for this method is long and detailed, so the easiest way to see it is to press *Shift + Tab* while your cursor is on it in the Jupyter Notebook.

We only need four of its arguments here:

```
sns.heatmap(confusion_train, annot=True, xticklabels=LABELS,
yticklabels=LABELS)
plt.xlabel("Predicted")
plt.ylabel("True")
```

Here, we get the following:

```
LABELS = ["negative", "positive"]
```

The code for displaying the confusion matrix for the test set is identical, apart from the use of the test set in place of the train set:

```
# Create a confusion matrix on test data.
confusion_test = tf.math.confusion_matrix(labels=test_df["polarity"],
predictions=get_predictions(estimator, predict_test_input_fn))
print(confusion_test.numpy())
# Normalize the confusion matrix so that each row sums to 1.
top = confusion_test.numpy()
bottom = np.sum(top)
confusion_test = 2*top/bottom
sns.heatmap(confusion_test, annot=True, xticklabels=LABELS,
yticklabels=LABELS);
plt.xlabel("Predicted");
plt.ylabel("True");
```

That concludes our examination of sentiment analysis for IMDb.

Summary

In this chapter, we looked at an Estimator for training the fashion dataset. We saw how Estimators provide a simple, intuitive API for TensorFlow.

We then looked at another application, this time for the sentiment classification of reviews of movies in the IMDb. We saw how TensorFlow Hub provides us with text embeddings, that is, vectors for words, which is where words with similar meanings have similar vectors.

In this book, we have seen an overview of TensorFlow 2.0 alpha.

Converting from tf1.12 to tf2

Google supplies a command-line script called `tf_upgrade_v2`, which converts version 1.12 files (both `.py` and `.ipynb` files) into TensorFlow 2 compatible files.

The syntax for this conversion is as follows:

```
tf_upgrade_v2   --infile  file_to_convert --outfile  converted_file
```

There is a demonstration of this upgrade script in action at `https://www.youtube.com/watch?v=JmSNUeBG-PQlist=PLQY2H8rRoyvzoUYI26kHmKSJBedn3SQuBindex=32t=71s`, and more detailed information regarding it is available at `https://github.com/tensorflow/docs/blob/master/site/en/r2/guide/upgrade.md`.

It is important to note that you should *not* update parts of your code manually *before* running this script.

The script will not fix all of the issues, but the report it produces will identify those issues that must be fixed manually.

In particular, `tf.contrib` has been removed from TF2 and so any calls to functions that used to live there must be tracked down and fixed manually.

Here is an example of the report that the script produces:

```
Processing file 'Chapter1_TF2_Snippets.ipynb'
 outputting to 'Chapter1_TF2_alpha'
---------------------------------------------------------------------
------

  37:4:  INFO: Added keywords to args of function 'tf.size'
  48:13: INFO: Added keywords to args of function 'tf.transpose'
  74:0:  INFO: Added keywords to args of function 'tf.reduce_mean'
  75:0:  INFO: Added keywords to args of function 'tf.reduce_mean'
  76:0:  INFO: Added keywords to args of function 'tf.reduce_mean'
  77:0:  INFO: Added keywords to args of function 'tf.reduce_mean'
  78:0:  INFO: Added keywords to args of function 'tf.reduce_mean'
  110:4: INFO: Added keywords to args of function 'tf.argmax'
  114:4: INFO: Added keywords to args of function 'tf.argmin'
  121:4: INFO: Added keywords to args of function 'tf.argmax'
  123:4: INFO: Added keywords to args of function 'tf.argmin'
  127:4: INFO: Added keywords to args of function 'tf.argmax'
  129:4: INFO: Added keywords to args of function 'tf.argmin'
  136:0: ERROR: Using member tf.contrib.integrate.odeint in deprecated
module tf.contrib. tf.contrib.integrate.odeint cannot be converted
automatically. tf.contrib will not be distributed with TensorFlow 2.0,
please consider an alternative in non-contrib TensorFlow, a community-
maintained repository, or fork the required code.
  162:10: INFO: Added keywords to args of function 'tf.transpose'
  173:11: INFO: Added keywords to args of function 'tf.reduce_mean'
```

Other Books You May Enjoy

If you enjoyed this book, you may be interested in these other books by Packt:

Deep Learning with TensorFlow - Second Edition
Giancarlo Zaccone, Md. Rezaul Karim

ISBN: 978-1-78883-110-9

- Apply deep machine intelligence and GPU computing with TensorFlow
- Access public datasets and use TensorFlow to load, process, and transform the data
- Discover how to use the high-level TensorFlow API to build more powerful applications
- Use deep learning for scalable object detection and mobile computing
- Train machines quickly to learn from data by exploring reinforcement learning techniques
- Explore active areas of deep learning research and applications

Intelligent Mobile Projects with TensorFlow
Jeff Tang

ISBN: 978-1-78883-454-4

- Classify images with transfer learning
- Detect objects and their locations
- Transform pictures with amazing art styles
- Understand simple speech commands
- Describe images in natural language
- Recognize drawing with Convolutional Neural Network and Long Short-Term Memory
- Predict stock price with Recurrent Neural Network in TensorFlow and Keras
- Generate and enhance images with generative adversarial networks

Leave a review - let other readers know what you think

Please share your thoughts on this book with others by leaving a review on the site that you bought it from. If you purchased the book from Amazon, please leave us an honest review on this book's Amazon page. This is vital so that other potential readers can see and use your unbiased opinion to make purchasing decisions, we can understand what our customers think about our products, and our authors can see your feedback on the title that they have worked with Packt to create. It will only take a few minutes of your time, but is valuable to other potential customers, our authors, and Packt. Thank you!

Index

CPSIA information can be obtained
at www.ICGtesting.com
Printed in the USA
LVHW102333190519
618428LV00004B/36/P

9 781789 530759